CHRISTMAS
Stitchery

Line drawings by Rosemary Lindsay

Photography by Peter Milner

CHRISTMAS
Stitchery

Over 40 projects to put the magic
back into Christmas

JENNY CHIPPINDALE
KATE THORP

A DAVID & CHARLES CRAFT BOOK

Typeset in Goudy by ABM Typographics Ltd
and printed in Italy
by New Interlitho SpA., Milan
for David & Charles Publishers plc
Brunel House   Newton Abbot   Devon

British Library Cataloguing in Publication Data
Chippindale, Jenny
  Christmas stitchery.
  1. Needlework. Christmas motifs
  I. Title II. Thorp, Kate
  746.4

ISBN 0–7153–9491–6

© Jenny Chippendale and Kate Thorp 1990

Distributed in the United States by
Sterling Publishing Co Inc,
387 Park Avenue South, New York, NY 10016-8810

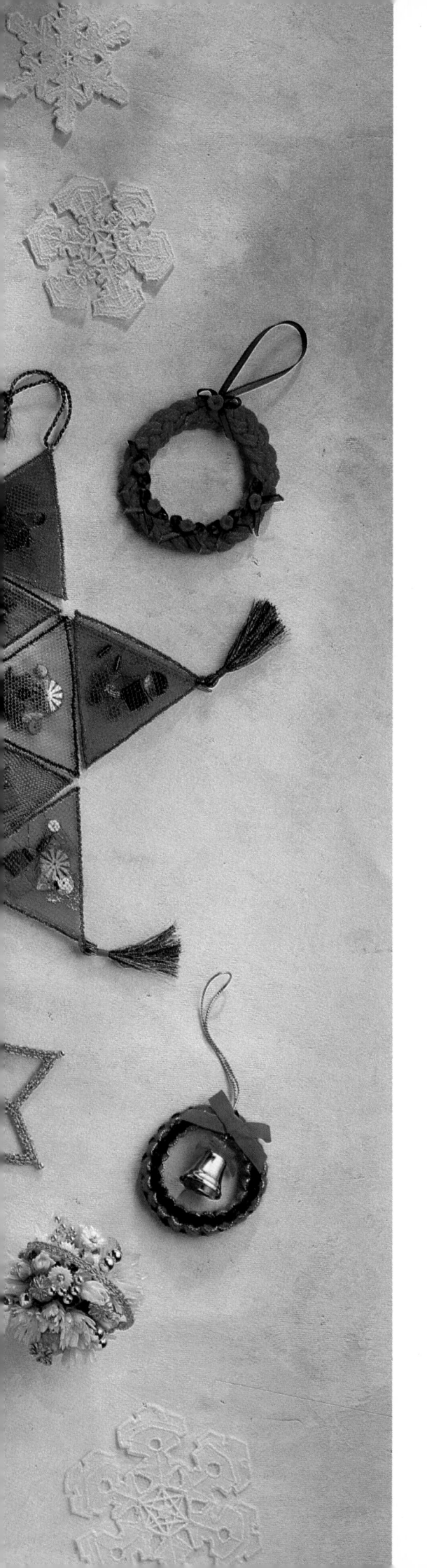

CONTENTS

INTRODUCTION

☆Put the magic back into Christmas with these lovely handmade decorations and cards for your family and friends. Christmas provides a wonderful opportunity for you to use your needlework skills. Beautiful decorations are a pleasure to make and hang each year and give a truly personal touch to this special festival. Indeed, they become heirlooms, carefully packed away on Twelfth Night and brought out amongst much family excitement the following December as the box is unpacked and the tree and home are decorated. New items can be added to the collection each year, to be treasured and enjoyed by future generations.

☆Anyone who receives a hand-stitched Christmas card will appreciate the care that has gone into its making and will feel very special. There is a delightful variety of cards here to suit every skill and taste.

☆How satisfying it is to make your own individual contribution to the festive season without the endless and often fruitless search through the shops for tasteful decorations and cards; it is easier on the purse too, and much more fun.

☆A child's Advent tree, individual stockings for the family, tree decorations, bird trees, wallhangings, a delicate snowflake mobile, these and many more will inspire you to bring warmth and style to Christmas with the magic of your needle.

HOW TO USE THE BOOK

☆A wide range of needlecraft skills is needed if you wish to make all the decorations and cards in this book. Some are very easy, involving only cutting out and a little simple stitchery. Others involve specialist skills such as crochet or free machine embroidery. This is not a crochet book or a book about free machine embroidery, but we have included projects which use these techniques. If you are a novice at any of the specialist crafts, do consult books that are devoted to those subjects. At the back of the book there is a short section on Techniques and Stitches which we hope will be helpful.

☆Read right through the instructions before beginning a project. If you have only basic needle skills, begin with the simpler projects but do not be afraid to try some of the more advanced ones. You may not be totally satisfied with your first efforts but don't be discouraged – have another go.

☆Actual size patterns are given wherever possible. It is worth taking the trouble to make very accurate templates.

☆Do not spoil your work with careless finishing or trimmings which are too heavy and clumsy. We urge you to use appropriate materials. This does not mean that you would never substitute other fabrics. For instance, the machine-quilted decorations might look gorgeous made with a beautiful brocade, in which case you would not quilt but would begin at the lining stage.

☆We have enjoyed designing and making the projects for this book. We hope it will give you great pleasure and many happy hours of creative Christmas stitchery.

☆*Happy Christmas!*

Tree
Decorations

CHRISTMAS ANGEL

This charming little angel can be placed at the top of the Christmas tree or alternatively she will stand on a table. Her head is a bead and the body a cone made of card covered with cream silk. Small pieces of different fabric stiffeners are used in her construction, so see what you or your friends can find in the scrap-bag.

•

APPROXIMATE HEIGHT

16cm (6¼in)

•

MATERIALS

20cm (¼yd) cream silk

Small quantities of:

White non-woven pelmet stiffener (eg pelmet or craft quality Vilene)

White non-woven lightweight fabric stiffener (eg Vilene)

White non-woven medium-weight iron-on fabric stiffener (eg Vilene)

Fusible web (eg Bondaweb)

30mm (1³⁄₁₆in) natural wooden bead

White pipe-cleaner cut to 15cm (6in)

Gold card

Flesh-coloured felt

Straw-coloured coton perlé

Gold metallic machine thread

Matt varnish

Black enamel paint

Fine paint-brush

PVA adhesive

Tracing paper and thin card for templates and cone

MAKING THE CONE FOR THE BODY SECTION

Trace the body pattern and make a template (see Techniques and Stitches, p143). The template can also be used for the cone. Draw round it onto a piece of medium-weight fabric stiffener. Cut out and iron onto the back of the cream silk following the grain direction shown on the pattern. Cut out the silk leaving 12mm (½in) turnings. Work some rows of machine stitchery around the hem of the skirt using gold metallic thread. A combination of zigzag and straight stitches look attractive. Position the card onto the back of the skirt and glue the turnings down all round. Ladder stitch the sides together to make a cone (see Techniques and Stitches, p142).

MAKING THE HEAD

Take the pipe-cleaner (cut to the given size) and fold in two. Insert the folded end into the bead and glue. Paint the head with matt varnish and, when dry, paint the face (Fig 1).

Fig 1 Detail showing face and hair

PREPARING THE HAIR

Cut some short lengths of coton perlé for a fringe. Draw a pencil line above the eyebrows as a guide. Put a dab of adhesive above this line and fix strands of 'hair' in place. Trim the fringe (Fig 1).

Cover the back of the head in the same way.

To complete the hair, make a winding card 8 x 9cm (3¼ x 3½in) and cut a 5mm (³⁄₁₆in) slit across the centre 3cm (1¼in) long (Fig 2).

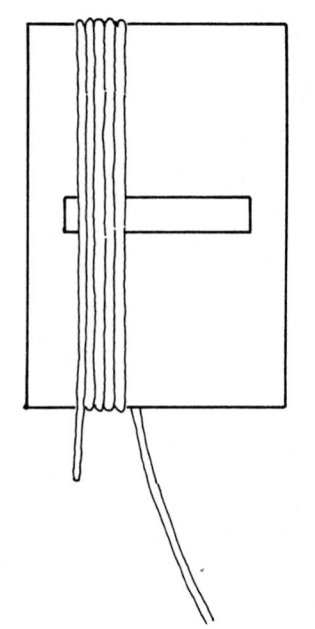

Fig 2 Winding card showing the slit across the centre (not to scale)

Use this to wind some coton perlé to a width of 2cm (¾in). With a matching thread, machine along the slit, running back over the stitches at both ends to secure. Cut the 'hair' away from the top and bottom of the card. Glue onto the head. Trim all ends.

Fix the head to the body section by gluing the pipe-cleaner inside the cone.

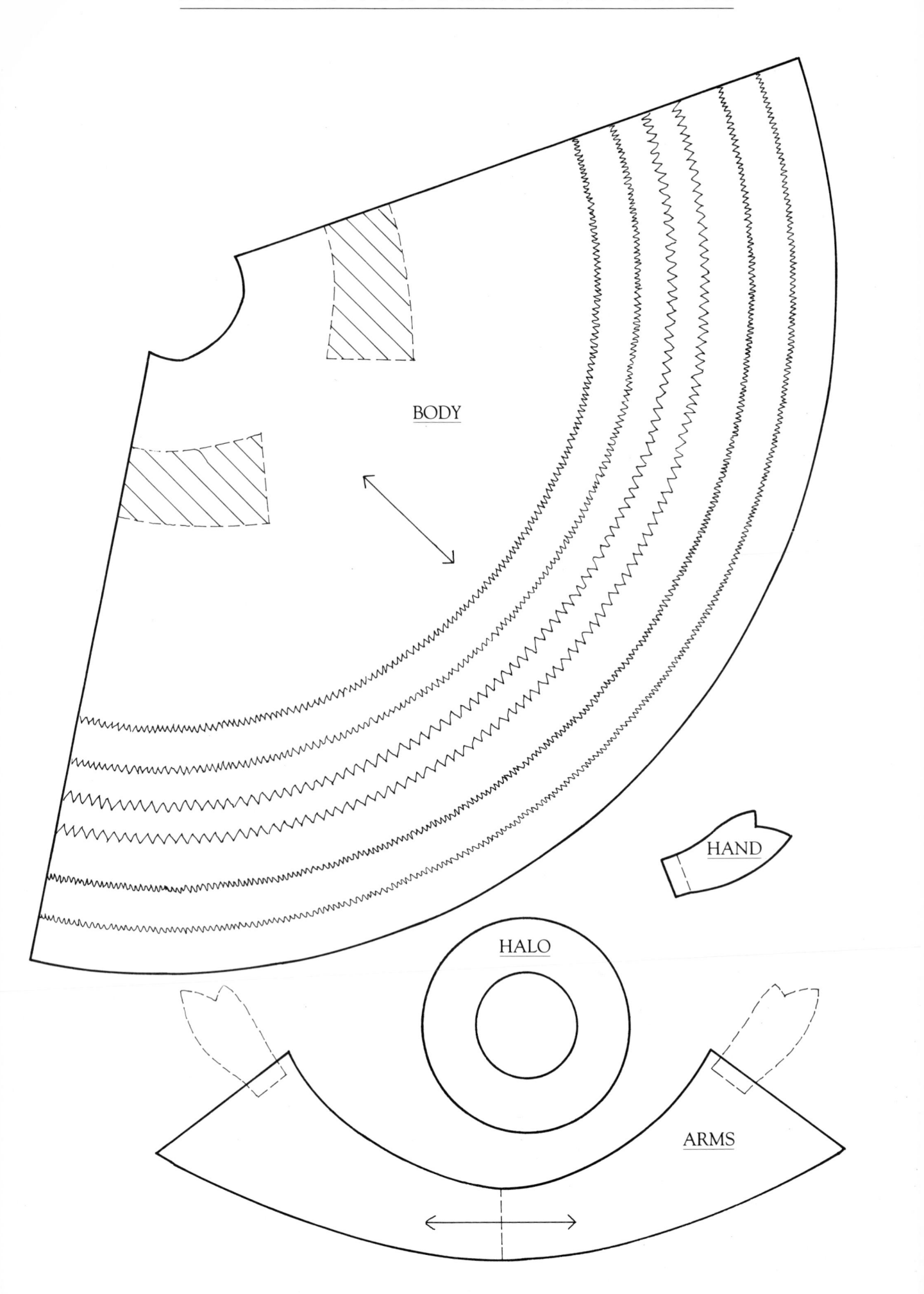

BODY

HAND

HALO

ARMS

WINGS

COLLAR

MAKING THE ARMS

Trace the pattern for the arms and make a template. Cut out one rectangle from both pelmet stiffener and fusible web 8 x 20cm (3 x 8in). Iron the adhesive side of the fusible web onto the pelmet stiffener (see manufacturer's instructions).

Place the template on the fused material, draw round it and cut out along the line. Peel the backing paper from the fusible web and iron the arms onto a piece of silk. Cut the arms out of the silk leaving 6mm (¼in) turnings round the fused materials.

Work a row of gold zigzag along the cuff edges. Glue turnings all round to the back.

Trace the pattern for the hands and make a template. Sandwich 2 pieces of flesh-coloured felt together with fusible web.

Draw round the template twice and cut out 2 hands. Glue these to the arms using the pattern as a guide.

The wrong side of the arms can be neatened with fabric stiffener. Using the template, cut out the fabric stiffener and iron it onto the back.

Glue the completed arms in position at the back of the body using the pattern as a guide.

Cut out the collar in lightweight fabric stiffener, position round the neck and oversew the edges together at the back.

Cut out a halo in gold card (or gold paper glued to white card). Glue in place on the head.

MAKING THE WINGS

Trace the pattern for the wings and make a template. Draw round and cut out in pelmet stiffener. Using the metallic thread, decorate with feathers of free machine stitchery (see Techniques and Stitches, p140). Set the machine for normal sewing and zigzag round the edge of the wings with the same thread. Glue or stitch onto the back of the angel.

Bring the hands together and hold in place with a few stitches.

COUNTED THREAD DECORATIONS

These three-sided decorations give you a chance to use some simple embroidery stitches. They are worked on an evenweave fabric, and a sparkle is obtained by using a lurex crochet thread.

•

SIZES

11.5cm (4½in) and 10cm (4in), without tassels

•

MATERIALS

23cm (¼yd) cream Aida fabric, 18 threads to 2.5cm (1in)

1 colour in coton perlé and 3 others in a lurex crochet thread, or any other heavy metallic thread, for each ornament

Tapestry needle

25cm (10in) or 12cm (5in) embroidery hoop

Thin card for mounting

PVA adhesive

Tracing paper

The decorations are three-sided, each side being worked the same in mainly straight stitch, with a central row of Rhodes stitches.

When using Aida fabric, follow the mesh of the coarse flat weave where holes are obvious. Each thread is actually made up of 4 fine threads in a group and stitches are worked from hole to hole.

EMBROIDERY CHART
(see the photograph for colour guidelines or choose your own)

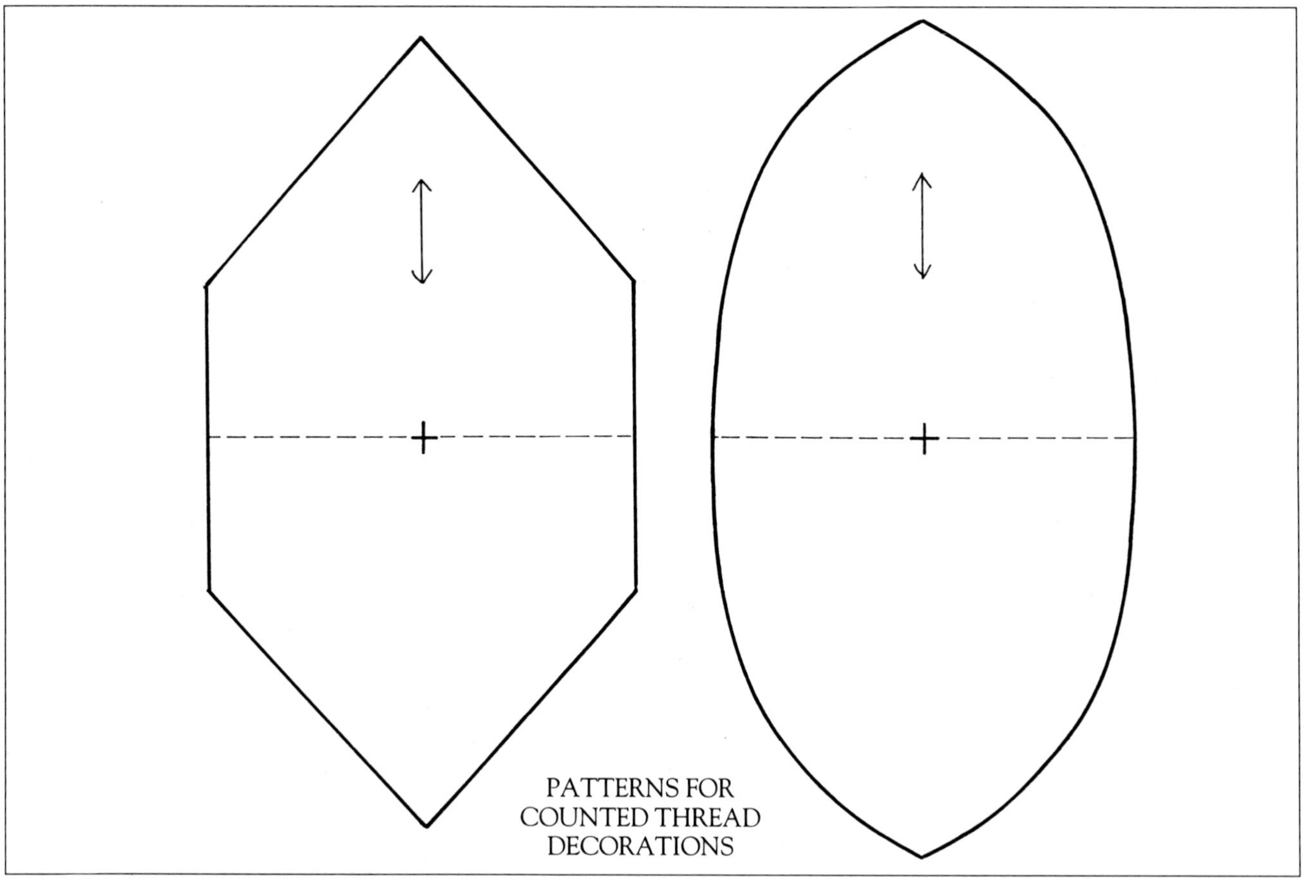

PATTERNS FOR
COUNTED THREAD
DECORATIONS

PREPARING THE FABRIC
FOR EMBROIDERY

Trace either pattern onto paper and cut out. Pin the paper pattern onto the fabric, following the grain, and baste round it leaving 10mm (³⁄₈in) allowance round each. Repeat twice more. If you are using the larger hoop, 3 shapes can be positioned beside each other on the fabric.

Mark the central point of each shape with a pin. Using the pin as a guide, follow the chart and work the embroidery.

Always start a line of stitches from the centre and work outwards.

A good tip is to work the rows of straight stitch first. The position is then set for the Rhodes stitches (Fig 1).

MAKING UP THE
DECORATION

Cut out the 3 embroidered sides leaving the required turnings. Use the pattern and cut out 3 sides in card (see Techniques and Stitches, p143). Carefully position a card onto the back of each embroidered piece. Glue the turnings down over the card. (It is easier to stitch the sides together if you keep the adhesive away from the very edge of the card.)

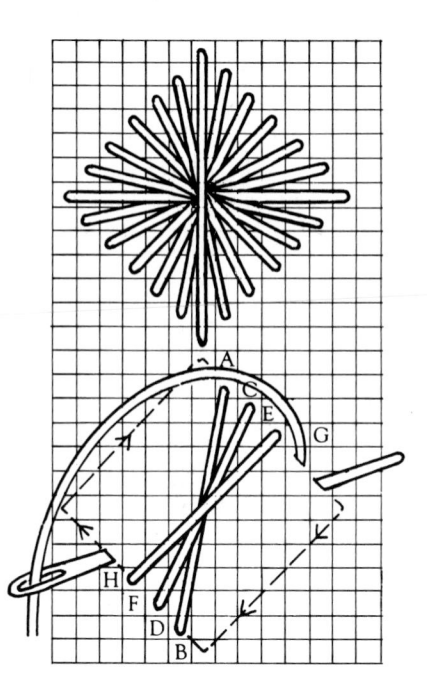

Fig 1 Rhodes stitch. Take the needle out at A, insert at B, out again at C and in at D. Continue round the four sides of the square

For the hanging loop cut a piece of the lurex thread 18cm (7in) long and knot the ends together.

With a cream sewing thread oversew or ladder stitch (see Techniques and Stitches, p142) the 3 sides together. As you complete the third side, insert the knotted end of the hanging loop into the top of the decoration. Secure with extra stitches.

Make a cord (see Techniques and Stitches, p143) using a 2½m (2¾yd) length of lurex thread. Begin at the top of the decoration and secure the unknotted end of the cord with several stitches. Slip stitch it down (see Techniques and Stitches, p142) over the seams in a continuous line ending at the bottom point. Oversew the cord here several times pulling the thread tightly to secure it. Cut off the surplus.

Make a tassel 7.5cm (3in) long (see Techniques and Stitches, p143) with threads used for the embroidery. Extra fine metallic threads wound into the tassel give a richer effect. Sew the finished tassel onto the bottom of the decoration.

DECORATED WALNUTS

Gold-painted walnuts, decorated with crocheted flowers and other trimmings, look very pretty hanging on the Christmas tree. Small artificial flowers can be used instead of the crocheted flowers.

MATERIALS

Walnuts (American walnuts are a more attractive shape than Chinese ones)

Bradawl (woodworking tool with a narrow chisel-like blade for making holes in the walnuts)

Alder cones or other small cones

Gold paint (small cans sold for painting models)

Plasticine and short sticks (optional)

Cream and gold crochet/ embroidery threads

1.25mm crochet hook

Gold and pearl beads (assorted sizes)

Beading wire

Leaf sequins

Cream ribbon 3mm (⅛in) wide

Thin gold cord

PVA adhesive

PREPARING THE WALNUTS

Make a hole in the centre top of the walnuts with a bradawl. Enlarge the natural hole where the two halves meet by gently breaking away the edge of the shell with the corner of the bradawl blade.

Give the walnuts 2 coats of gold paint. Allow the first coat to dry before applying the second. If you push a short stick into the walnut hole the nut is easier to hold. The sticks can easily be split from a small piece of wood (cocktail sticks are too thin). Stand the sticks in a lump of Plasticine while the paint is drying.

DECORATING THE WALNUTS

Prepare a selection of the following trimmings:

Cord or ribbon loops (Fig 1).   Placing the thumb and little finger of your left hand about 6.5cm (2½in) apart, wrap thin cord or narrow ribbon round them 3 times in a figure-of-eight movement. Wrap a piece of beading wire about 7.5cm (3in) long round the centre of the loops and twist tightly.

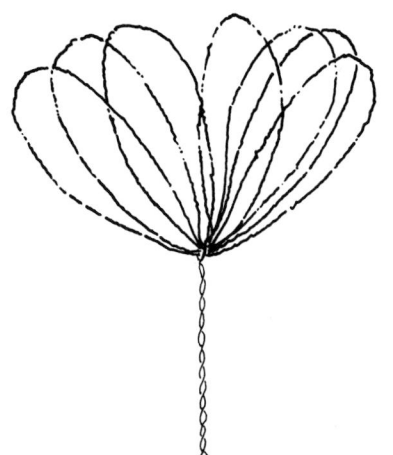

Fig 1 Cord loops

Twist the ends of the wire together.
Bead loops (Fig 2).   The beads are 'back-stitched' onto beading wire (Fig 3). Cut a piece of wire approximately 36cm (14in) long. Thread the wire through a small bead until the bead is about 5cm (2in) from one end. Thread the wire through the bead again in the same direction and pull the wire tight round the bead.

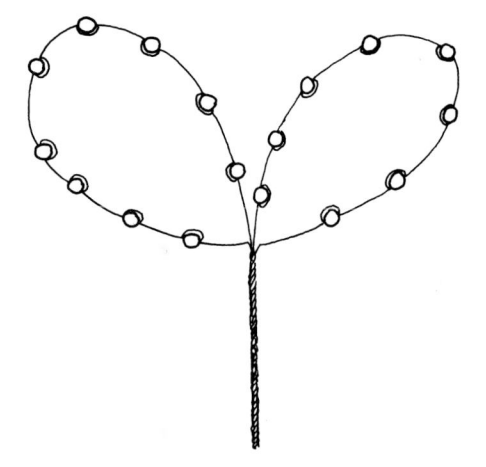

Fig 2 Bead loops

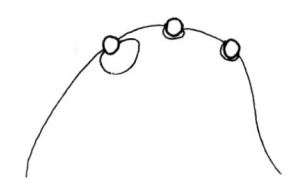

Fig 3 'Back-stitching' beads onto wire

Continue adding beads, spacing them at random along the wire, until the distance between the first and the last bead is about 15cm (6in). Twist the wire to form 2 bead loops and twist the ends together to form a stem approximately 4cm (1½in) long. Cut the ends of the wire.
Bead stems (Fig 4)   Cut a piece of beading wire approximately 10cm

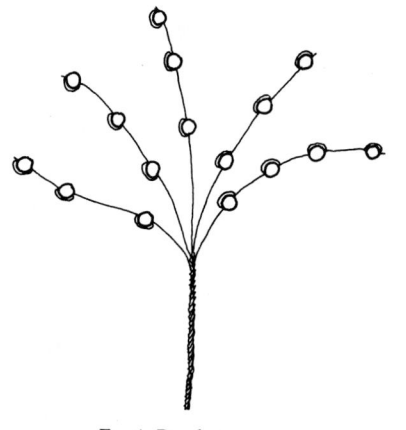

Fig 4 Bead stems

(4in) long for each stem. 'Back-stitch' 3 or 4 small beads at random on one half of the wire. Twist 3 or 5 stems together to form a spray.

Bead clusters (Fig 5)   Cut a piece of wire approximately 40cm (16in) long. Thread the first bead onto the wire until it is about 6cm (2½in) from one end. Twist the wire round the bead and continue twisting for about 2cm (¾in) to make a stem. Thread the second bead onto the long end of the wire until it is about 2cm (¾in) away from the base of the first stem. Twist the wire to form a second stem.

Continue adding beads, varying the length of the individual stems slightly, until the cluster is the required size.

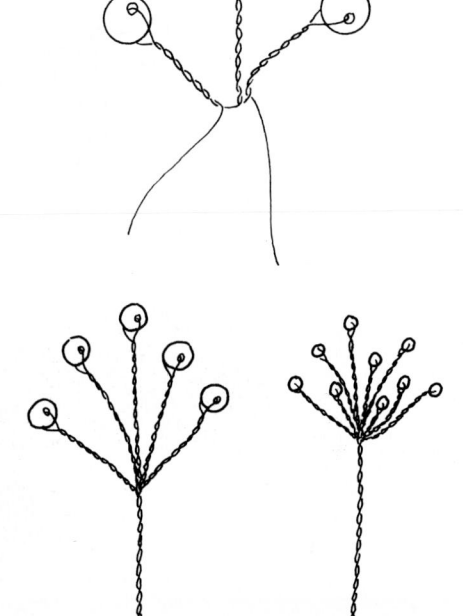

Fig 5 Bead clusters

Twist the ends of the wire together to form a stem approximately 4cm (1½in) long. Cut the ends of the wire.

A piece of wire approximately 40cm (16in) long will make a cluster of 7 small beads with individual stems approximately 1.2-2cm (½-¾in) long. Adjust the length of the wire for clusters of a different size.

Small cones (Fig 6)   Paint the tips of the cone petals gold and leave to dry. Wrap beading wire round the petals at the base of the cone and twist the ends together to form a stem about 4cm (1½in) long. If the cone is too big, break off a few rows of petals at the base of the cone and cut the central core to about 6mm (¼in) before adding the wire. Small poppy seed-heads can be used instead of cones.

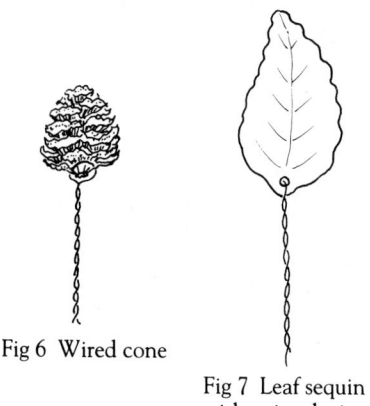

Fig 6 Wired cone

Fig 7 Leaf sequin with twisted wire stem

Leaf sequins (Fig 7)   Thread beading wire through the hole at the base of the leaf and twist the ends together to form a stem 4cm (1½in) long.

CROCHETED FLOWERS

For crochet stitches and abbreviations, see Techniques and Stitches, p139. All the flowers are finished in the same way. Fasten off and darn the ends in neatly. Sew a bead to the centre of the flower. Thread beading wire through the bead and take both ends through the centre of the flower to the back. Twist the ends of the wire together to form a stem.

Vary the flowers by using different threads. The finer the thread the smaller the flowers will be.

Flower A Ch 5, sl st in 1st ch to form a ring.
Round 1: (Ch 4, sl st in ring), 8 times.
Flower B Ch 5, sl st in 1st ch to form a ring.
Round 1: (Ch 2, 1 tr in ring, ch 2, sl st in ring), 5 or 6 times.
Flower C Ch 5, sl st in 1st ch to form a ring.
Round 1: (Ch 3, 1 dtr in ring, ch 3, sl st in ring) 5 or 6 times.
Flower D Ch 5, sl st in 1st ch to form a ring.
Round 1: Ch 3 (counts as 1st tr), *ch 4, sl st in 4th ch from hook, 1 tr in ring. Repeat from *3 times. Ch 4, sl st in 4th ch from hook, sl st in 3rd of beg 3 ch.
Flower E Ch 5, sl st in 1st ch to form a ring.
Round 1: Ch 3 (counts as 1st tr), 8 tr in ring, sl st in 3rd of beg 3 ch.

COMPLETING THE WALNUTS

Cut a piece of narrow cream ribbon or thin gold cord 18cm (7in) long. Tie the ends together and dab a little adhesive on the knot. Push the knot into the hole in the top of the walnut.

Arrange a few flowers and other trimmings in the walnut (Fig 8). You will often find that the wire stems lock together and stay in place without any adhesive. Squeeze a little adhesive into the hole if necessary.

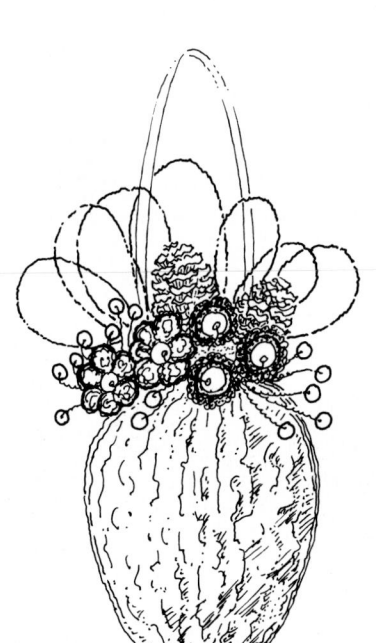

Fig 8 Completed walnut

MACHINE-QUILTED DECORATIONS

These elegant decorations are designed to hold a special little gift. They are machine quilted with gold thread using automatic decorative stitches.

•

APPROXIMATE SIZE

HEART 9cm (3½in)
FAN 10cm (4in)
STOCKING 11cm (4½in)

•

MATERIALS

Cream silk or satin:
HEART 25 x 14cm (10 x 5½in)
FAN 34 x 15cm (13½ x 6in)
STOCKING 28 x 24cm (11 x 9½in)
Cotton backing (old sheets will do)
Lightweight polyester wadding (batting)
Cream lining fabric
Gold metallic machine thread
Cream machine thread
Fine gold cord
6mm (¼in) wide gold ribbon or plain braid for handle and bows
Tracing paper and thin card for templates
Water-erasable pen

MACHINE QUILTING

The quilting consists of 3 layers, the top fabric, wadding and backing fabric, which are sandwiched together and machined with decorative stitches. Press the top and backing fabrics before you begin.

Lay the backing fabric on a smooth surface with the wadding on top. Place the top fabric right side up on the wadding (Fig 1).

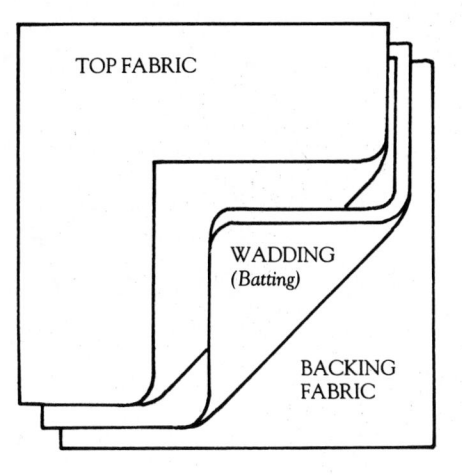

Fig 1 Making a quilting 'sandwich'

Pin the 3 layers together round the edge, smoothing the fabrics as you work. Basting is unnecessary on such a small piece of quilting. Check the backing fabric to make sure that it is smooth.

Read your machine manual to see if there are special instructions for machine quilting.

Use fine gold metallic machine thread in the top of your machine and cream machine thread on the spool.

Work a test piece to check the tension and use a new machine needle. Work the rows of stitching in the same direction using the edge of the presser foot to space the rows.

If your machine cannot do automatic decorative stitches, interesting patterns can be worked using just straight stitch and zigzag (see Advent Tree, p63). Mix rows of straight and zigzag stitching. Vary the width and length of the zigzag stitches and the spaces between the rows.

Specific instructions about the size to be quilted and the way the rows are to be worked are given for each decoration.

MAKING THE HEART

Trace the pattern and make a template (see Techniques and Stitches, p143).

Cut a piece of backing fabric, wadding and top fabric 25 x 14cm (10 x 5½in). Make a sandwich with the fabrics and pin round the edge.

The rows of machine stitching are worked along the length of the fabric. Use gold metallic thread in the top of the machine and cream machine thread on the spool. Work the first row 2.5cm (1in) down from the top long edge. Continue working parallel rows of decorative stitches until the band of stitching is approximately 8cm (3in) deep.

Draw round the template twice on the back of the quilting – this is the stitching line. Add a 12mm (½in) seam allowance all round. Cut out the 2 hearts from the quilting and 2 hearts from the lining fabric.

Place the quilting and lining right sides together and pin round the edge. With cream thread sew round the heart using a small machine stitch, leaving an opening for turning as shown on the pattern. Make the second heart in the same way.

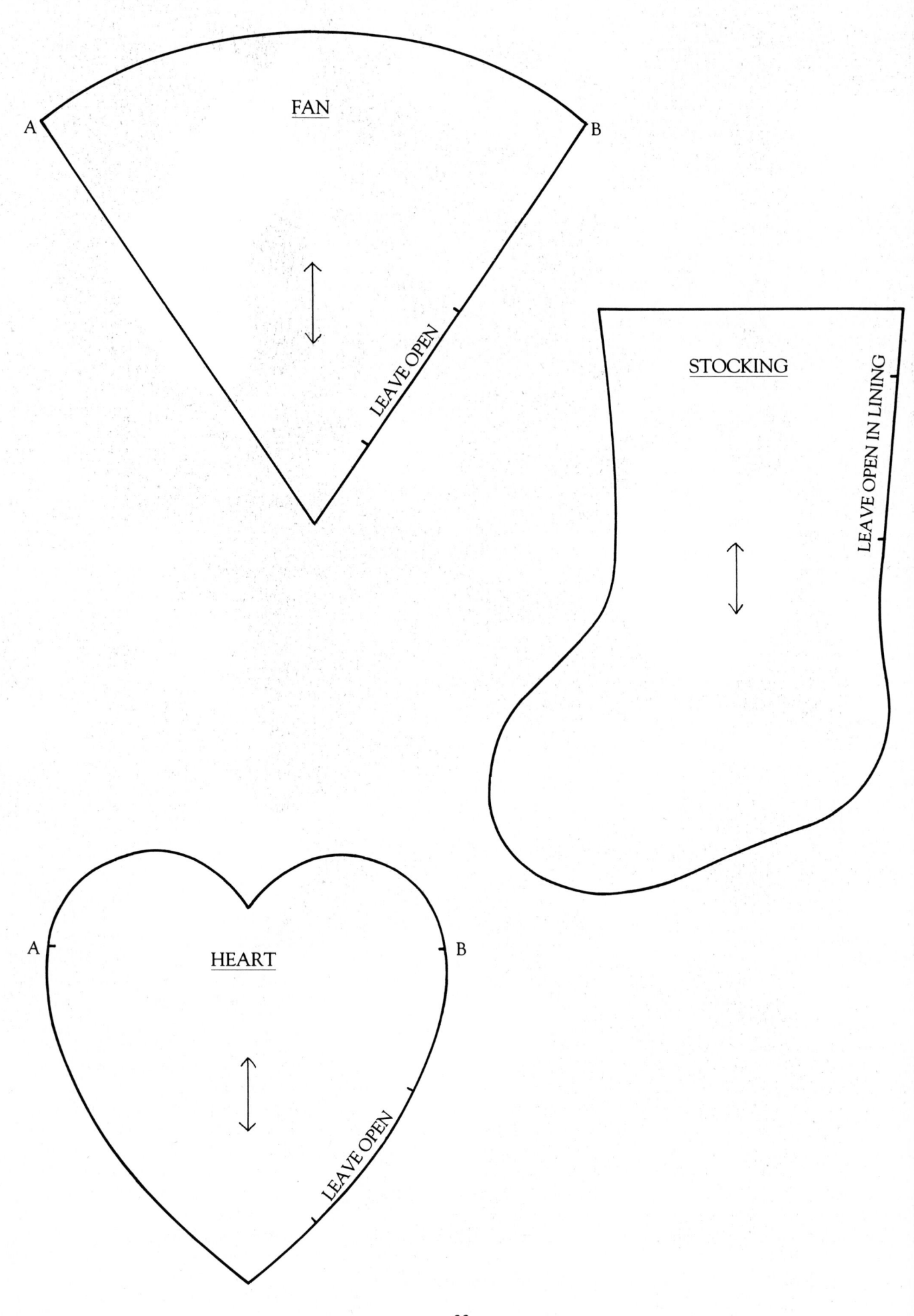

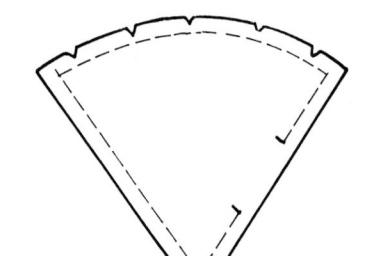

Fig 2 Heart and fan showing the seam
allowance with curves and points clipped

Unpick the quilting stitches in the seam allowance and trim the wadding and backing close to the stitching line. Trim the top fabric and lining to about 6mm (¼in) and clip the curves and the point at the base (Fig 2). Turn right side out and ladder stitch the opening (see Techniques and Stitches, p142).

With wrong sides together, slip stitch the 2 hearts along the seam line from A to B, leaving the top open.

Thin gold cord is used to trim the seams and top edges of the heart. Use fine gold thread to sew on the cord. Begin the stitching at the centre top of the heart where the ends of the cord will be hidden by the bow. Sew on cord all round the heart. Sew cord along the other top edge beginning at point A and finishing at point B. Tuck the ends of this cord into the decoration.

Cut a piece of stiff gold ribbon or plain braid 18cm (7in) long. Stitch the ends to the centre top of each side of the heart to form a handle. Make 2 neat bows and stitch 1 to each side to cover the ends of the handle and cord.

MAKING THE FAN

The rows of decorative stitching on the fan are curved and run parallel to the top edge.

Trace the pattern and make a template.

Using a water-erasable pen draw round the template twice on the right side of the top fabric. Add a 2.5cm (1in) seam allowance all round and cut out both fans. Extend the curved lines at the top of the fans to the edges of the fabric. Cut 2 pieces of wadding and backing fabric the same size. Matching the curved top edges, make a sandwich with the backing fabric, wadding and top fabric (right side up). Pin the 3 layers together round the

edges, smoothing the fabrics as you work. Follow the curved line on the top fabric for the first row of decorative machine stitching (use gold thread in the top of the machine, and cream thread on the spool). Continue with parallel rows, using the edge of the presser foot as a guide, until the fabric is covered. Stitch to the edge of the fabric on each row.

Work the second piece of quilting to match the first (use a different combination of stitches if you wish).

Remove the erasable pen lines with a damp cloth.

Draw round the template on the back of both pieces of quilting, matching the curved top of the template to the curve of the stitching – this is the stitching line. Add a 12mm (½in) seam allowance all round. Cut the 2 fans from the quilting and 2 fans from the lining fabric.

Complete the fan, following the instructions for making the heart (see above).

MAKING THE STOCKING

Trace the pattern and make a template.

To avoid a seam at the top of the stocking, the lining and stocking are cut from the same piece of top fabric (Fig 3).

Cut a piece of backing fabric and a piece of wadding 5 x 24cm (2 x 9½in) and a piece of top fabric 28 x 24cm (11 x 9½in).

Place the 2 short edges of the top fabric together and press the fold. Open out and place right side down on a smooth surface. Make a sandwich by placing the wadding and then the backing on top with one long edge about 1cm (⅜in) over the centre fold. Pin round the edge of the 3

layers. Turn the sandwich over and transfer the pins to the right side, smoothing the fabrics as you pin.

Work a 3cm (1¼in) band of decorative machine stitching (gold thread in the top of the machine, cream on the spool) over the 3 layers. Begin the first row just below the centre fold.

Carefully trim the wadding and backing close to the stitching.

Use a fine pencil to draw round the template twice on the back of the work. Match the top of the template to the fold and remember to reverse the template to make a pair. Mark the lining by again reversing the template and matching the top edge to the fold (Fig 3) – the pencil line is the stitching line. Add a 12mm (½in) seam allowance and cut out.

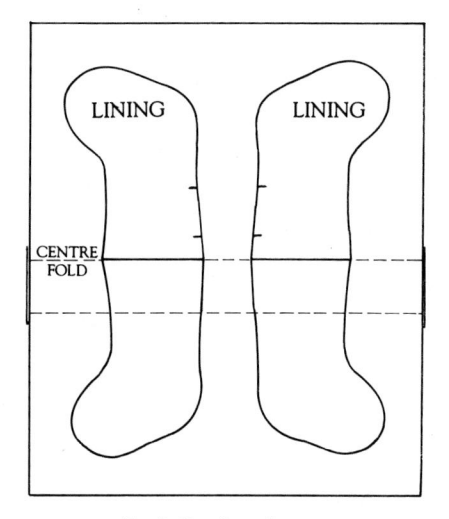

Fig 3 Stocking layout

Place right sides together, matching the stitching line, and pin round the edge. Sew round on the pencil line using a small machine stitch and cream thread. Leave an opening in the lining for turning as shown on the pattern.

Unpick the quilting stitches in the seam allowance and carefully trim the wadding and backing close to the stitching. Trim the seam allowance to about 6mm (¼in) and clip the curves. Turn right side out and slip stitch the opening in the lining.

Press carefully and push the lining inside the stocking.

Attach a gold hanging loop to the top back of the stocking, tucking the ends of the loop inside the stocking.

PLAITED WREATHS

The wreaths are made from simple three-fold plaits (hair plaits) decorated with crocheted or guipure flowers and felt leaves. The plaits are made from cord or string which is stiff enough to hold its shape when plaited and formed into a ring or tear-drop shape. Natural string looks attractive with the red and green flowers but it can be dyed if a different colour is required.

•

APPROXIMATE SIZE

7cm (2¾in)

•

MATERIALS

String or cord

Matching thread

PVA adhesive

Guipure flowers and fabric dye if necessary

OR crochet cotton and a 1.25mm hook

Green felt

Beads

Narrow ribbon or thread for hanging loop

Macramé board or other board which will take pins easily

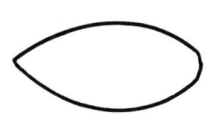

Pattern for leaf

MAKING THE WREATHS

The aim is to make a flat plait about 1cm (⅜in) wide. Experiment with different thicknesses of cord. Use 2 or 3 cords, lying side by side, for each fold (Fig 1). This is better than using 1 thick cord which would make a bulky plait.

Cut 3 cords approximately 75cm (30in) long and fold in the centre. Place the centre of the cords round a pin stuck in a macramé board (6 cords in all). Bring the 2 left-hand cords to the middle and then bring the 2 right-hand cords to the middle. Continue until the plait measures about 20cm (8in). As you work make sure that the cords lie side by side and that the plait remains flat.

If you use 3 cords in each fold you will need 4 cords approximately 75cm (30in) long and an extra cord about 45cm (18in) long. Lay the short cord

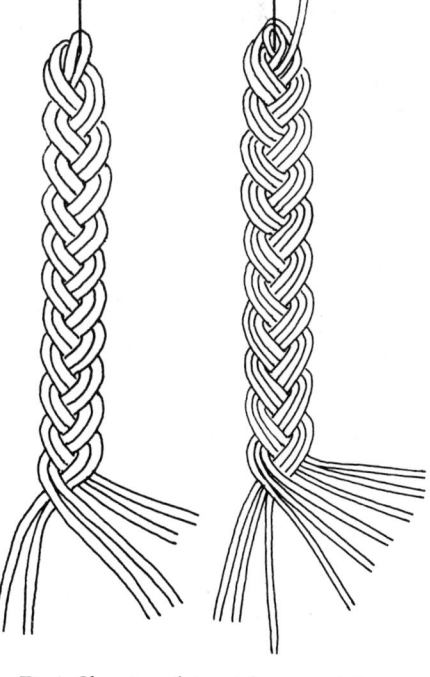

Fig 1 Showing plaits with two and three cords in each fold

beside the others that have been placed round the pin, with a few centimetres (inches) sticking out at the top (9 cords in all).

Use a little adhesive or a few stitches to secure the loose ends of the plait before forming it into a circle or tear-drop shape. Overlap the ends of the plait and stitch through both layers as neatly as possible using matching thread. Trim the ends of the cords. Make sure that the join is hidden when you attach the flowers.

DECORATING THE WREATHS

Use crocheted flowers (see instructions below) or guipure flowers which are sold by the metre (yard) in haberdashery shops and market stalls. If you cannot find red or green guipure flowers, dye white ones with fabric dyes. Dip white flowers in weak tea if you wish to make cream and gold wreaths.

Sew the flowers to the wreaths. Sew a bead to the centre of each flower. If you wish to add leaves cut simple leaf shapes from green felt and stitch in place before adding the flowers.

The wreaths can also be decorated with bows made from narrow ribbon with small crocheted motifs stitched to the bows (see below).

Add a hanging loop of thread or narrow ribbon.

CROCHET FLOWER

For crochet stitches and abbreviations see Techniques and Stitches, p139.

Ch 4, sl st in 1st ch to form a ring.

Round 1: (Ch 4, sl st in ring) 6 times. Fasten off and darn ends in neatly.

CROCHET MOTIF

Ch 4, sl st in 1st ch to form a ring.

Round 1: Ch 3 (counts as 1st tr), 8 tr in ring, sl st in 3rd of beg 3ch. Fasten off and darn ends in neatly.

FINGER-KNITTED WREATHS

A finger-knitted cord, decorated with gold thread, is used to make these attractive wreaths. A brass bell is suspended in the centre of the wreath and a red bow hides the join in the cord.

APPROXIMATE SIZE

6½cm (2½in)

•

MATERIALS

Approximately 4mm (³⁄₁₆in) diameter green and red rug wool or cord

Gold crochet thread or thin gold cord

Brass bell approximately 2cm (¾in) diameter

6mm (¼in) wide red ribbon

Red or green sewing cotton

FINGER KNITTING

For finger knitting, 2 pieces of contrasting wool are required, about 5 times the length of the finished cord.

Tie a slip knot on the red wool (Fig 1). Tie the ends of the red and green wool together (Fig 2).

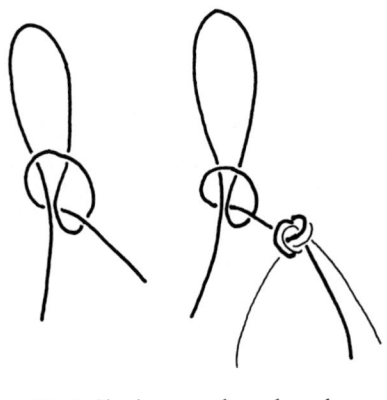

Fig 1 Slip knot on the red wool

Fig 2 Tie ends of red and green wool together

Place the slip knot loop (red) on the forefinger of the right hand. Hold the knot between the thumb and second finger with the long end of the wool held against the palm of the hand with the little finger.

Hold the green wool between the thumb and second finger of the left hand with the long end held against the palm with the little finger.

Bring the forefinger of the left hand in front of the red loop (Fig 3) and insert it into the loop. Both forefingers should now be pointing in the same direction.

Hook up the green wool with the tip of the left forefinger. Pull up the green wool to form a loop on the left forefinger. Drop the red loop over the green one and transfer the knot to the left hand. Pull the long end of the red wool downwards to tighten (Fig 4).

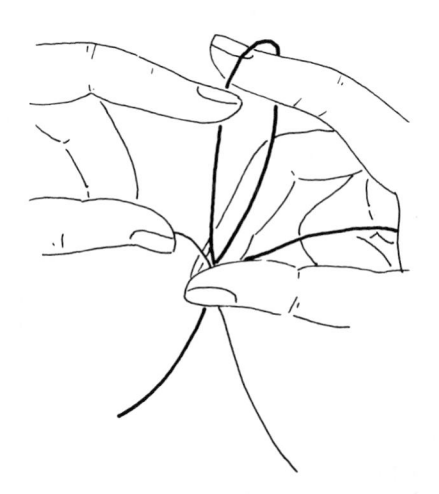

Fig 3 Bring forefinger of left hand in front of red loop. Insert finger in loop and hook up the green wool

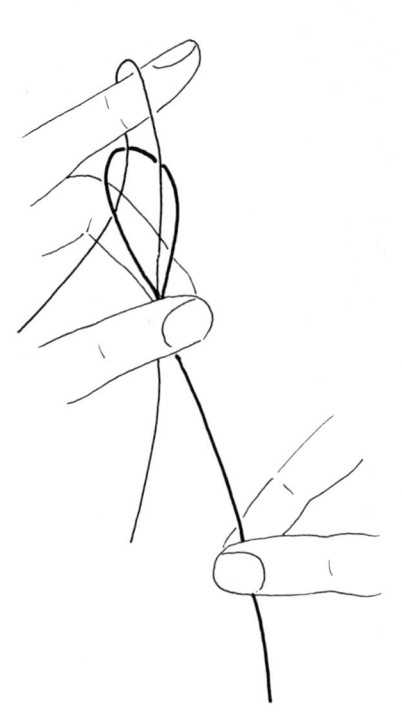

Fig 4 Green loop now on left forefinger. Pull red wool downwards to tighten

Bring the right forefinger in front of the green loop and insert it into the loop. Both forefingers should again be pointing in the same direction. Hook up the red wool with the tip of the right forefinger. Pull up the red wool to form a loop on the right forefinger. Drop the green loop over the red one and transfer the knot to the right hand. Pull the long end of the green wool downwards to tighten.

Continue finger knitting on the left and right forefingers until the cord is 18cm (7in) long.

Note: The loop on the forefinger should be big enough to insert the other forefinger. The yarn should be pulled downwards when tightening and the tension kept as even as possible.

MAKING THE WREATHS

Make a finger-knitted cord 18cm (7in) long. The front of the cord has green in the centre with red on each side. Try to make the central green 'stitches' and the red border even.

Secure each end of the cord by neatly stitching through all the strands of wool to prevent them from unravelling. Cut off the beginning knot and trim the ends of the wool.

Form into a ring by overlapping the ends of the cord by about 12mm

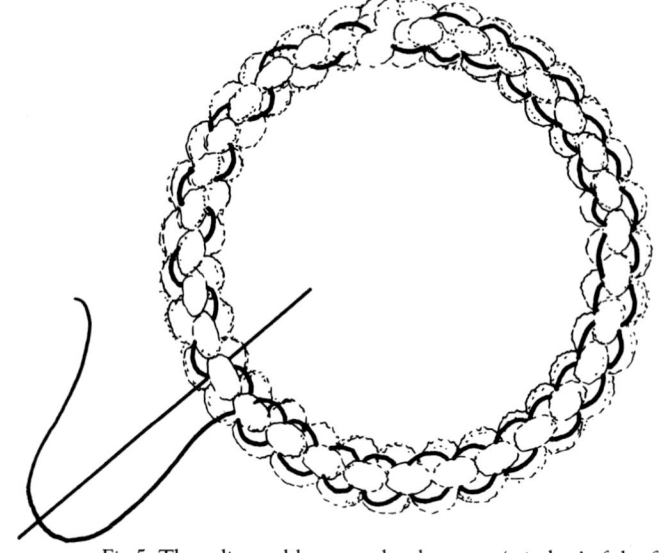

Fig 5 Threading gold yarn under the green 'stitches' of the finger cord

(½in) and stitching through both layers. Make the join as neat as possible. The front of the join will be hidden by a ribbon bow.

Decorate by threading gold crochet yarn or thin cord under the green 'stitches' in the centre of the finger-knitted cord (Fig 5). Beginning at the join with a small back stitch, take the gold thread under one 'stitch' and back through the next in the opposite direction.

Continue threading in and out of the green 'stitches' until you reach the beginning. Work a second row of

gold, taking the thread under each 'stitch' in the opposite direction to the first row. You will then have loops of gold on each side of the front of the cord. Fasten off neatly.

Tie gold thread to the ring at the top of the bell. Stitch the ends of the thread to the wreath at the join so that the bell is suspended in the centre of the wreath.

Tie a bow with the red ribbon and stitch it to the wreath over the join.

Attach a hanging loop of gold thread to the wreath above the centre of the bell.

Completed wreath

SUFFOLK PUFF DECORATIONS

Suffolk puffs (yo-yos) are used to make these elegant tree decorations. Suffolk puffs are gathered circles of fabric. Fine silks or velvet and inexpensive silky lining fabrics are ideal – heavier fabrics cannot be gathered up tight enough. Christmas cotton prints can be used and look attractive, but they do not have the elegance of the richer fabrics.

•

APPROXIMATE SIZE

SINGLE PUFF 7cm (2¾in)
DOUBLE PUFF 12cm (4¾in)

•

MATERIALS

Fine rich fabrics:
SINGLE PUFF 13 x 26cm (5 x 10in)
DOUBLE PUFF 19 x 19cm (7½ x 7½in)

Matching thread

White non-woven pelmet stiffener
(eg pelmet or craft quality Vilene) –
optional

Selection of the following trimmings:
Beads ⎫
Sequins ⎪
Pretty buttons with shanks ⎪
Fine thread ⎬ gold/silver
Crochet thread ⎪
Thin cord ⎪
Narrow lace or braid ⎭

1.25mm crochet hook

Tracing paper and thin card for templates

MAKING THE PUFFS

Trace the patterns and make templates (see Techniques and Stitches, p143). Draw round the templates on the back of the fabric. Cut out 2 circles for the single decoration and 2 of each size for the double one. Do not add a seam allowance.

Turn a 6mm (¼in) hem to the wrong side. Work a row of running stitches round the edge using strong thread and beginning with a knot and small back stitch (Fig 1). Pull the thread up tight but do not fasten off (Fig 2).

Flatten the puff with your fingers and measure across. Cut a pelmet stiffener circle the exact size of the puff. The size will vary according to the fabric used and the size of the running stitches. Place the circle inside the puff. Pull the gathering thread up tight making sure that the gathered edge is in the middle. Fasten off neatly and securely. Lining with stiffener is not essential but it gives a crisper edge. Thin card could be used but a hole would need to be made in the centre so that the trimmings could be stitched in place.

Make a matching puff and slip stitch them together round the edge. Leave a 6mm (¼in) gap so that a hanging loop and the ends of the edging cord or braid can be tucked in. You will need 2 pairs of puffs for the double decoration.

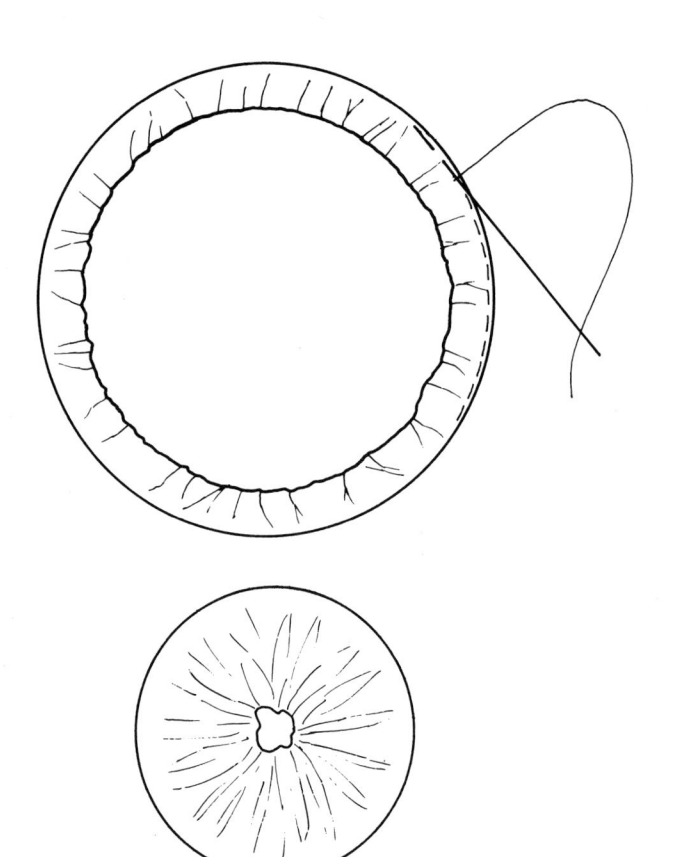

Figs 1 and 2 Making a Suffolk Puff

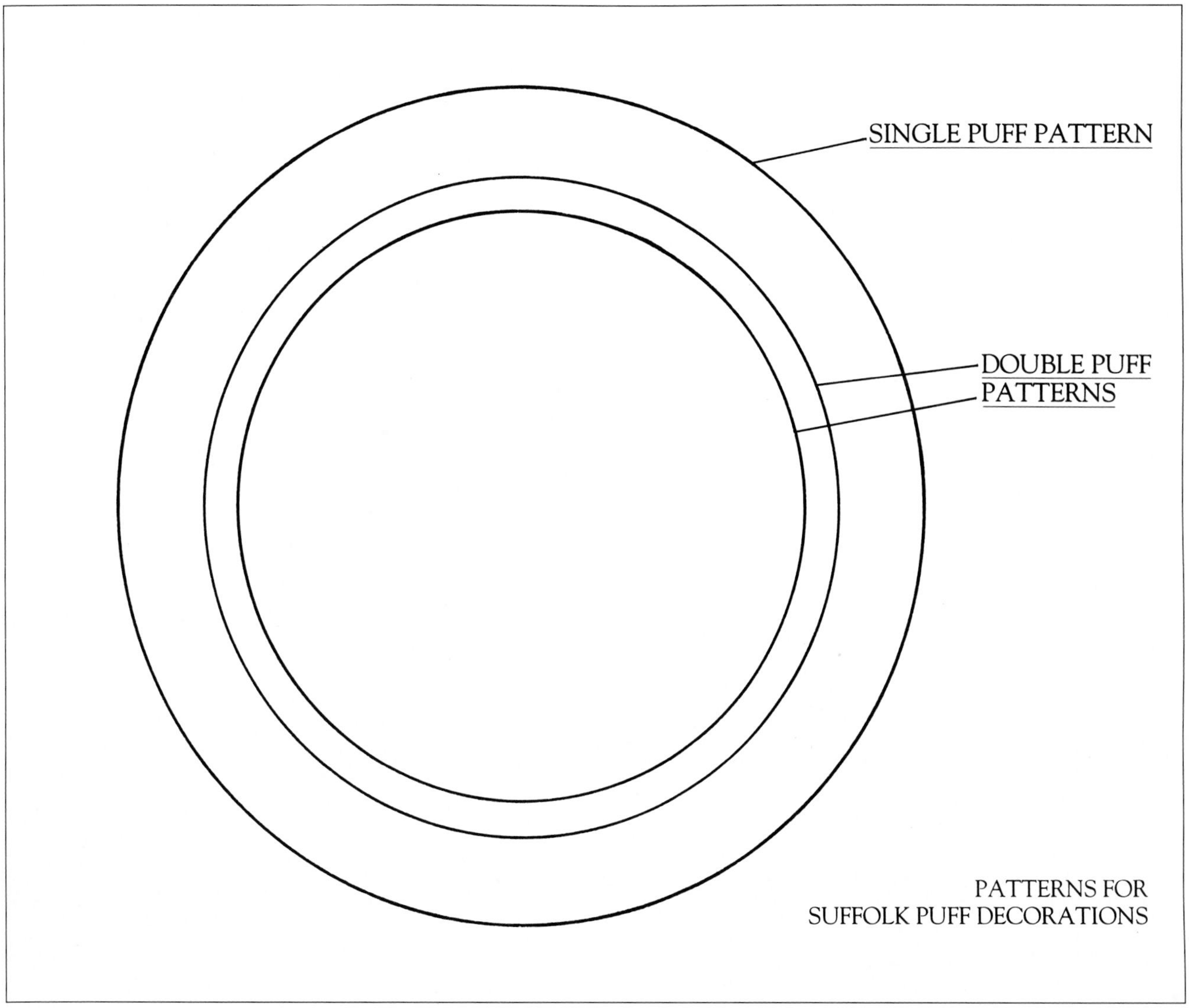

SINGLE PUFF PATTERN

DOUBLE PUFF PATTERNS

PATTERNS FOR
SUFFOLK PUFF DECORATIONS

Fig 3 Completed Double Puff Decoration

DECORATING THE PUFFS

Slip stitch a twisted cord (see Techniques and Stitches, p143), narrow lace or crocheted picot edging (see below) round the edge of the puffs. Tuck the ends in between the puffs in the gap left for the purpose. Insert a hanging loop (in larger puff only of the double decoration) and slip stitch the gap. Sew pretty buttons or crocheted motifs (see below) to the centres of the puffs.

For the double decoration, join the 2 pairs of puffs together by working 2 tiny neat back stitches in the edge opposite the hanging loop. Pass the thread through 2 or 3 beads and then work 2 tiny back stitches in the edge of the smaller puff. Add a tassel (see Techniques and Stitches, p143) or a few beads to the bottom of the small puff.

CROCHETED PICOT EDGING

For crochet abbreviations and stitches, see Techniques and Stitches, p139.

*Ch 4, sl st in 3rd ch from hook, repeat from * until the edging is the required length.

CROCHETED CENTRAL MOTIF

Ch 6, sl st in 1st ch to form a ring.

Round 1: Ch 1, (ch3, 1 dc in ring) 8 times. Fasten off and darn the ends in neatly.

CROCHETED SNOWFLAKES

hese delicate snow-
flakes look lovely
hanging on the Christmas
tree. They are inexpensive to
make and require only a few
yards of crochet cotton. They
could be made into an
attractive mobile.

APPROXIMATE SIZE

10cm (4in)

MATERIALS

Coats crochet cotton No 10 or
other fine white crochet cotton

1.25mm crochet hook

White granulated sugar

OR laundry starch

Rust-proof pins

Piece of polystyrene (often used
in packaging)

OR board which will take pins easily

Transparent plastic bag

Small clean brush

Transparent nylon thread

Tracing paper

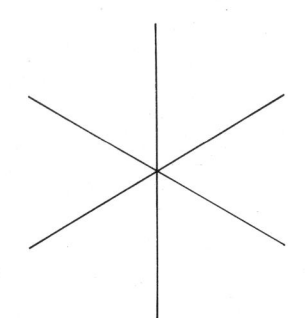

Fig 1 Blocking guide

GENERAL INSTRUCTIONS

For crochet abbreviations and
stitches, see Techniques and Stitches,
p139.

All rounds are worked on the right
side – do not turn the work. A rather
tight tension gives the most
satisfactory result; loose, loopy
stitches will spoil the effect. Use a
smaller hook if your tension is loose.
Keep the tension as even as possible.

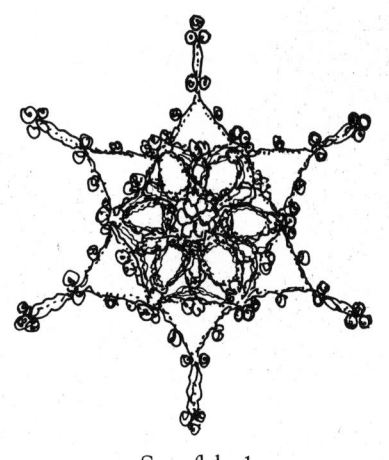

Snowflake 1

SNOWFLAKE 1

Ch 6, sl st in the 1st ch to form a ring.
Round 1: Ch 3 (counts as 1st tr), 1
tr in ring, (ch 2, 2 tr in ring) 5 times,
ch 2, join with a sl st in the 3rd of the
beg 3 ch.
Round 2: Sl st to the 1st 2 ch sp of
rnd 1, ch 3 (counts as 1st tr), ch 2, 1
tr in same 2 ch sp, *ch 6, (1 tr, ch 2,
1 tr) in next 2 ch sp, repeat from *4
times. Ch 6, join with a sl st in the
3rd of the beg 3 ch.
Round 3: Sl st in the 1st 2 ch sp of
rnd 2, *(3 dc, 3 ch, 3 dc) in next 6 ch
1p, sl st in next 2 ch sp (ch 5, sl st in
5th ch from hook) twice (2 picots
made), sl st in same 2 ch sp. Repeat
from *5 times.
Round 4: Sl st to 1st 3 ch sp of rnd
3, *(ch 5, sl st in 5th ch from hook) 3

times, sl st in same 3 ch sp, ch 9, sl st
in 5th ch from hook, ch 8, dc in 5th
ch from hook, ch 5, (ch 5, sl st in 5th
ch from hook) 3 times, ch 10, sl st in
5th ch from hook, sl st in dc, ch 8, sl
st in 5th ch from hook, ch 4, sl st in
next 3 ch sp. Repeat from *5 times.
Fasten off and darn ends in neatly.

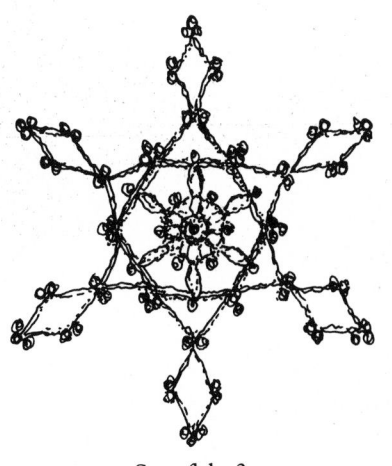

Snowflake 2

SNOWFLAKE 2

Ch 6, sl st in the 1st ch to form a ring.
Round 1: Ch 3 (counts as 1st tr), ch
4, sl st in 4th ch from hook, 1 tr in
ring. *Ch 2, 1 tr in ring, ch 4, sl st in
4th ch from hook, 1 tr in ring. Repeat
from *4 times. Ch 1, 1 htr in 3rd of
beg 3 ch.
Round 2: Ch 4 (counts as 1st dtr),
ch 4, sl st in 4th ch from hook, 1 dtr
in htr sp. *Ch 6, 1 dtr in next 2 ch sp
of rnd 1, ch 4, sl st in 4th ch from hook,
1 dtr in same 2 ch sp. Repeat from
*4 times. Ch 3, 1 tr in 4th of beg 4 ch.
Round 3: *Ch 9, dc in 4th ch from
hook, (ch 7, sl st in 4th ch from hook,
ch 4, sl st in 4th ch from hook) twice,
(ch 4, sl st in 4th ch from hook, ch 7,
sl st in 4th ch from hook) twice, sl st
in dc, ch 5, 1 dc in centre of next 6 ch
1p, (ch 4, sl st in 4th ch from hook) 3
times, sl st in dc. Repeat from *5
times. Sl st in 1st ch at beg of rnd.
Fasten off and darn ends in neatly.

Snowflake 3

SNOWFLAKE 3

Ch 6, sl st in the 1st ch to form a ring.

Round 1: Ch 3 (counts as 1st tr), (ch 3, 1 tr in ring) 5 times. Ch 3, join with a sl st in the 3rd of the beg 3 ch.

Round 2: (2 dc, ch 2, 2 dc) in each 3 ch sp of rnd 1, join with a sl st in 1st dc.

Round 3: Sl st to 1st 2 ch sp of rnd 2, (ch 7, sl st in next 2 ch sp) 6 times.

Round 4: (4 dc, ch 2, 4 dc) in each 7 ch 1p of rnd 3, sl st in 1st dc.

Round 5: Sl st to 1st 2 ch sp of rnd 4. *Ch 3 (ch 5, 1 tr in 3rd ch from hook, ch 2, sl st in same 3rd ch) 7 times. Ch 5, sl st in same 2 ch sp, ch 4, 1 dtr in same 2 ch sp, ch 3, 1 tr in 3rd ch from hook, ch 2, sl st in same 3rd ch, 1 dtr in next 2 ch sp of rnd 4, ch 4 sl st in same 2 ch sp. Repeat from *5 times working in each 2 ch sp of previous rnd.

Fasten off and darn ends in neatly.

BLOCKING AND STIFFENING

If you are making several snowflakes it is a good idea to make them all first and stiffen them at the same time. You will find the blocking guide helpful when pinning out (Fig 1). One blocking guide will be needed for each snowflake.

Trace the guide a number of times onto greaseproof or tracing paper, extending the lines to the size of your snowflakes. The size will vary according to your tension and thread. Use a ruler to make accurate guides. Place the tracing on the polystyrene or board and cover with a plastic bag.

If necessary, wash the snowflakes in warm soapy water and rinse well. Remove excess moisture with a clean towel or kitchen paper.

Mix 4 tablespoons of white granulated sugar with 2 tablespoons of water in a small saucepan. Put the pan on a low heat and stir the solution until the sugar has dissolved. Leave to cool.

With right sides up, pin the damp snowflakes to shape using rust-proof pins. Matching the guide-lines, pin the centre first and then the points. Make sure the picots are in the correct positions.

Use a clean brush to coat the snowflakes thoroughly with the sugar solution. Mop up any surplus solution from the plastic with kitchen paper. Leave to dry. Remove pins before the snowflakes are completely dry or you may find that the pins will stick to the snowflakes and be difficult to take out.

If you prefer to use laundry starch, mix following the manufacturer's directions. Immerse the clean, dry snowflakes in the starch solution. Squeeze out surplus solution and pin out on the board (see above).

Tie one end of a piece of fine nylon transparent thread to a point on the snowflake, and tie a hanging loop at the other end.

CROCHETED STARS

These gold and silver stars are very easy to crochet. Only three basic stitches are used. The stars can be left plain or enriched with beads.

•

APPROXIMATE SIZE

LARGE STAR 11cm (4½in)
SMALL STAR 6cm (2½in)

•

MATERIALS

Twilley's Goldfingering or other metallic crochet thread

2.00mm crochet hook

Laundry starch

Rust-proof pins

Piece of polystyrene (often used in packaging)

OR board which will take pins easily

Transparent plastic bag

Fine gold or silver thread

Beads or sequins (optional)

Tracing paper

GENERAL INSTRUCTIONS

For crochet abbreviations and stitches, see Techniques and Stitches, p139.

All rounds are worked on the right side – do not turn the work. The double crochet in rounds 3 and 5 are worked into each chain stitch and not into the chain loop. If the chains in rounds 2 and 4 are too tight, the double crochet will be difficult to work. Use a larger hook for rounds 2 and 4 if your tension is tight. Make the chains as even as possible.

LARGE AND SMALL STARS

Fasten off after round 3 for small stars.

Ch 6, sl st in 1st ch to form a ring.

Round 1: Ch 3 (counts as 1st tr), 1 tr in ring, (ch 3, 2 tr in ring) 5 times, ch 3, sl st in 3rd of beg 3 ch.

Round 2: Sl st to centre of 1st 3 ch sp of rnd 1. (Ch 9, sl st in next 3 ch sp) 6 times.

Round 3: *1 dc in each of 1st 4 ch of 9 ch lp, (1 dc, ch 2, 1 dc) in 5th ch, 1 dc in each of next 4 ch. Repeat from *5 times, sl st in 1st dc.

Round 4: Sl st to 1st 2 ch sp of rnd 3, (ch 17, sl st in next 2 ch sp) 6 times.

Round 5: *1 dc in each of 1st 8 ch of 17 ch lp, (1 dc, ch 2, 1 dc) in 9th ch, 1 dc in each of next 8 ch. Repeat

from *5 times, sl st in 1st dc.

Fasten off and darn the ends in neatly.

BLOCKING AND STIFFENING

Follow the crocheted snowflakes instructions (see p34) for blocking and stiffening. Use laundry starch not the sugar solution. Use the snowflake blocking guide when pinning out.

DECORATING THE STARS

Sew on the beads or sequins with fine matching thread.

Stitch small beads to the tips of the stars. Suspend beads in the spaces by back stitching them onto thread (see Hearts and Stars, p38). Use fine matching thread to make a hanging loop on one of the points.

CROCHETED BASKETS

These simple baskets are very easy to crochet. Filled with small dried or artificial flowers they look very attractive hanging on the Christmas tree.

·

APPROXIMATE SIZE

5.5cm (2¼in) diameter

MATERIALS

Twilley's Goldfingering or other metallic gold crochet thread

Fine matching thread

2.00mm and 3.00mm crochet hooks

Laundry starch

Small piece of thin card

Piece of polystyrene (often used in packaging)

OR board which will take pins easily

Plastic bag

Rust-proof pins

Dried flower foam

Small dried or artificial flowers

Beads (optional)

Beading wire (optional)

GENERAL INSTRUCTIONS

For crochet stitches and abbreviations, see Techniques and Stitches, p139. Use a larger hook if your tension is tight. To make larger baskets, work

extra rounds for the base, increasing by 12 stitches in each round. Make the sides taller by repeating round 5 more times to give the required height. Finish the basket with rounds 8 and 9.

BASKET

Using a 2.00mm crochet hook, ch 4, sl st in 1st ch to form a ring.

Round 1: Ch 3 (counts as 1st tr), 11 tr in ring, sl st in 3rd of beg 3 ch (12sts).

Round 2: Ch 3 (counts as 1st tr), 1 tr in same place, 2 tr in each tr of rnd 1, sl st in 3rd of beg 3 ch (24sts).

Round 3: Ch 3 (counts as 1st tr), 1 tr in same place, (1 tr in next tr, 2 tr in next tr) 11 times, 1 tr in last tr of previous rnd, sl st in 3rd of beg 3 ch (36sts).

Round 4: Work under back loop only in this round. Ch 3 (counts as 1st tr), 1 tr in each tr of previous rnd, sl st in 3rd of beg 3 ch.

Round 5: Ch 3 (counts as 1st tr), 1 tr in each tr of previous rnd, sl st in 3rd of beg 3 ch.

Rounds 6 and 7: Work as rnd 5.

Round 8: Ch 3 (counts as 1st tr), 1 tr in same place, *1 tr in next tr, 2 tr in next tr. Repeat from * to end of rnd. 1 tr in last tr, sl st in 3rd of beg 3 ch.

Round 9: Picot edging: *ch 3, sl st in each of next 2 tr. Repeat from * to end of rnd.

Fasten off and darn the ends in neatly.

HANDLE

Using a 3.00mm crochet hook, make a chain 20cm (8in) long. Change to a 2.00mm hook and work 1 sl st in each ch, 3 sl st in 1st ch, 1 sl st in each ch, working back up the opposite edge of the chain (1 row of sl st on each side of the chain). Fasten off and darn the ends in neatly.

STIFFENING THE BASKETS

Cut circles of thin card to fit the bases of the baskets. It is a good idea to starch one basket first to test the stiffening qualities of the starch. If you find the basket is not stiff enough, use a stronger solution.

Mix hot water laundry starch, following the manufacturer's instructions. Immerse the baskets and handles in the starch. Squeeze to remove excess starch. Wipe off any starch remaining on the surface with a damp cloth.

Place a card circle in the base of each basket. Pull into shape making sure that the basket is round and the sides curve gently outwards.

Cover the polystyrene or board with the plastic bag. Stretch and pin the handles to the board. Leave to dry completely. Sew the ends of the handles to the inside of the basket with fine matching thread.

Cut a piece of dried flower foam to fit inside each basket and arrange the flowers. Bead clusters are an attractive addition if artificial flowers are used (see Decorated Walnuts, p18).

THREE SIMPLE TREE DECORATIONS

These simple decorations are very easy and quick to make. All you have to do is to cut out the shapes and add a few beads and sequins.

•

APPROXIMATE SIZE

7cm (2¾in)

•

MATERIALS

White non-woven pelmet stiffener (eg pelmet or craft quality Vilene): 18 x 24cm (7 x 9½in) will make 6 decorations

Fine silver thread

Silver beads and star sequins

Tracing paper and thin card for templates

MAKING THE DECORATIONS

Trace the patterns on p40 and make templates (see Techniques and Stitches, p143).

Draw round the template on the pelmet stiffener using a fine pencil. Cut out carefully. Curved scissors are helpful when cutting difficult inward curves. Cut out 3 holly leaves for the candle decoration.

FINISHING THE DECORATIONS

Sew a star sequin and hanging loop to the top of the trees using fine silver thread. Sew small star sequins or beads to the branches.

Sew a group of 3 holly leaves to the base of the candle and add 3 or 4 silver beads for the holly berries (Fig 1). Make a hanging loop at the top of the decoration with fine silver thread.

Fig 1 Showing the position of holly leaves and berries

HEARTS AND STARS

Crisp white pelmet stiffener is used to make these charming hearts and stars. Two layers are bonded together and decorated with tiny silver beads and sequins. Some of the hearts are also decorated with automatic machine stitching using silver thread. These decorations would also look pretty against a window. Use threads of varying lengths to make an attractive arrangement.

APPROXIMATE SIZE

HEARTS 9cm (3½in)
STARS 10cm (4in)

•

MATERIALS

White non-woven pelmet stiffener (eg pelmet or craft quality Vilene):
HEART 18 x 9cm (7 x 3½in)
STAR 21 x 10.5cm (8½ x 4in)
Fusible web (eg Bondaweb)
Small shiny transparent beads
Small silver beads and star sequins
Silver machine thread

MAKING THE HEARTS AND STARS

Trace the patterns on p40 onto the smooth side of fusible web and iron onto the pelmet stiffener. Cut out the heart/star carefully. Curved scissors are helpful when cutting difficult inward curves.

Remove the paper backing and iron the heart/star onto another piece of pelmet stiffener, using a damp cloth and dry iron. If you are adding decorative machine stitching do so at this stage (see photograph). Cut out the second layer of stiffener carefully.

DECORATING THE HEARTS AND STARS

The centres of the hearts and stars have beads and sequins strung across them on fine silver thread. The beads are held in place by back-stitching them onto the thread (Fig 1).

Begin with 1 or 2 back stitches in the back of the heart/star near the edge of the centre space. Push the needle through the edge of the centre space and pass the thread through a bead and back through again in the same direction. The bead can now be pushed into place but will not move on its own. Repeat with 2 or 3 more beads on the same thread. Work 1 or 2 back stitches in the back of the opposite edge. (See Figs 1 and 2 for the placement of beads and threads.) It is important to keep the thread taut across the space without distorting the shape. Take the needle between the layers of stiffener to the next position on the edge of the centre space and work 1 or 2 back stitches in the back before you continue to back stitch more beads onto the thread.

When all the beads are in place, sew star sequins to the pelmet stiffener if required. Add a silver hanging loop to a point on the star or to the centre top of the heart.

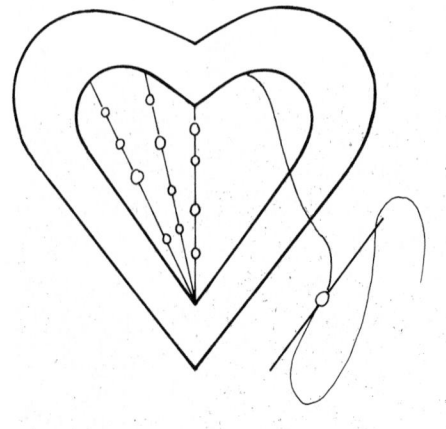

Fig 1 'Back-stitching' a bead onto thread

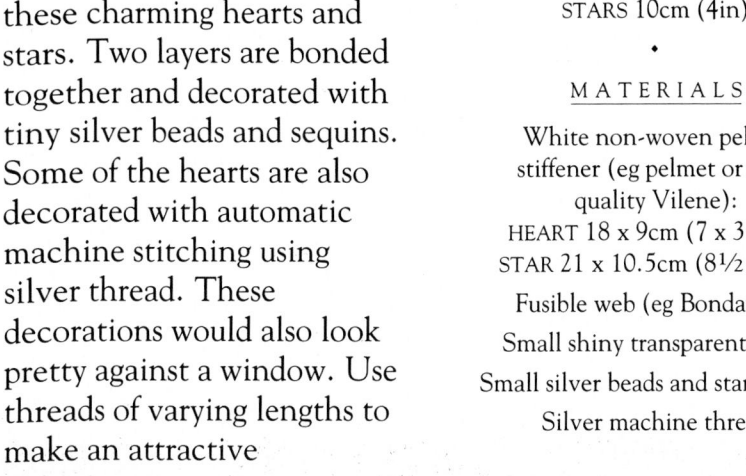
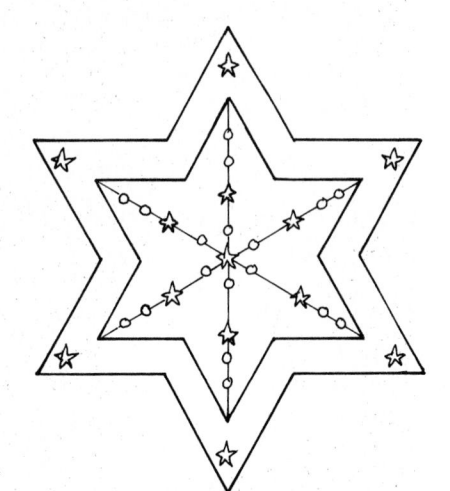

Fig 2 Alternative designs for the star

Wallhangings and Mobiles

STAR HANGING

This richly reflective hanging consists of twelve triangles assembled together to make a star. Each triangle is a parcel made with transparent fabrics sandwiched round a collection of sequins and small fragments of brightly coloured fabrics. Free machine stitchery is used to fix the 'treasures' in place and the completed star is decorated with multi-coloured tassels.

•

APPROXIMATE SIZE

27cm (10½in)

•

MATERIALS

Coloured nets

Various coloured transparent fabrics (organzas)

Sequins of varying colours and shapes

Scraps of richly coloured fabric

Tailor's chalk

13cm (5in) embroidery hoop

PVA adhesive

Metallic machine embroidery threads

Coloured threads for tassels

2 thin wooden rods for support

Tracing paper and thin card for template

Kitchen paper

Gold or silver metallic paint

Piece of polystyrene (often used in packaging)

OR board which will take pins easily (macramé board)

Plastic bag

MAKING THE PARCELS

Each parcel consists of 3 pieces of fabric 18cm (7in) square, 2 of different coloured net and 1 of organza.

Try to make each parcel different. Experiment with different colour combinations of nets and organzas and you will find that subtle variations can be achieved. Trace the triangular pattern and make a template (see Techniques and Stitches, p143).

Prepare the parcels on a flat surface. Place the template onto the square of organza and draw round it with tailor's chalk. Pin the organza to a layer of net.

The 'treasures' are different coloured and shaped sequins and small fragments of richly coloured fabrics. Position a few of these in the centre of the triangle and cover with a second layer of net. Pin closely round them to hold in place. (Basting is not successful at this stage as the 'treasures' move out of position as you stitch.)

Carefully place the square in an embroidery hoop ready for free machine stitchery (see Techniques and Stitches, p140).

Thread your machine with metallic thread on top and on the spool. Using

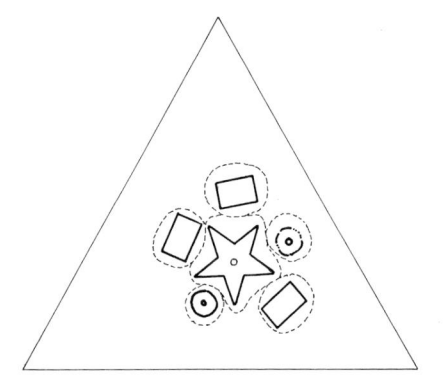

Fig 1 Free machining round the 'treasures' to fix in place

a straight stitch, machine round the 'treasures', taking out the pins as you go. Work slowly so that you do not break the needle on the pins (Fig 1).

A good tip is to use the tip of your embroidery scissors to hold the occasional sequin in place as you machine. They do like to jump out of position!

COMPLETING THE TRIANGLE

Take the work out of the hoop. Set the machine up for normal sewing and, using a metallic thread and straight stitch, machine round the triangle on the chalk line. Go over the straight stitch with a close zigzag. Cut surplus fabric away close to the

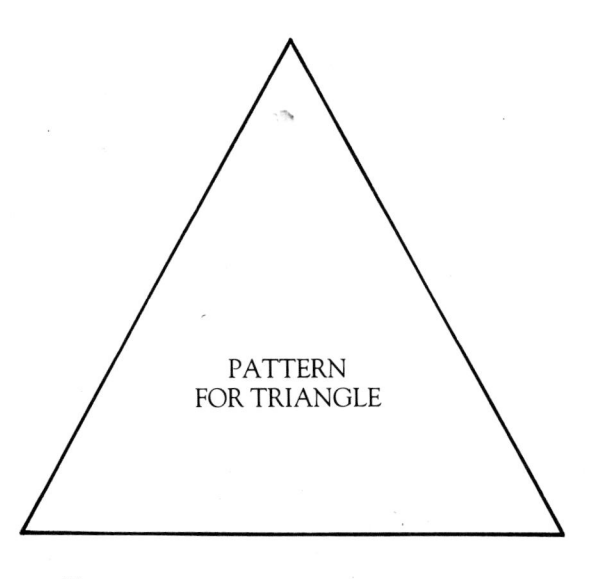

PATTERN
FOR TRIANGLE

stitching and the parcel is complete.

The 12 finished parcels are stiffened in a solution of 1 part adhesive added to 5 parts water. Immerse the parcels in the solution. Lift them out and pat them well with kitchen towel. Pin them out on a blocking board, covered with a plastic bag, and leave until dry.

ASSEMBLING THE HANGING

Make a full-size tracing of the star using the template and the illustration provided as a guide (Fig 2).

Place the tracing on the blocking board.

Cut a 30cm (12in) square of pale coloured net and pin this round the edges over the tracing. Now position the completed parcels onto this. Pin onto the net using the tracing as a guide.

Lift the hanging off the board and, using a metallic thread, work running stitches round each parcel, through the net, just inside the zigzagged edge.

Cut away the surplus backing net close to the running stitches.

Make 6 tassels 4cm (1½in) long (see Techniques and Stitches, p143) using a variety of threads – for example, embroidery threads, sewing cottons, metallic threads etc. Each tassel can be predominantly one colour. Attach these to the positions shown (Fig 2).

Make a twisted cord 25cm (10in) long (see Techniques and Stitches, p143), using different coloured threads. Attach the centre of the cord to the point at the top of the star. Bring the ends together. Knot and trim off the surplus.

Strengthen the back of the hanging at the widest points with two fine

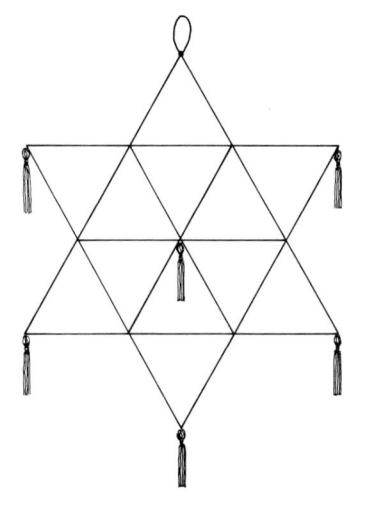

Fig 2 Guide showing position of triangles and tassels

wooden rods painted with metallic paint. (The thinnest available indoor plant support sticks are ideal for this.) Stitch over the rods neatly several times at the corners of the triangles.

THREE KINGS

The three kings on this hanging are worked in appliqué. The fabrics used for the robes are silks, and a fine cotton is used for the heads and hands. You can, of course, choose any coloured fabrics, but here is a guide for the three kings illustrated.

COLOUR

A Gold
B Turquoise
C Fine stripe
D Pink
E Gold metallic fabric
F Brown

•

APPROXIMATE SIZE

61 x 46cm (24 x 18in)

MATERIALS

25cm (9in) gold-coloured silk
25cm (9in) turquoise silk
25cm (9in) fine striped silk
20cm (8in) pink silk
10cm (4in) square gold metallic fabric (the gold silk will do)
20cm (8in) square brown cotton fabric
1m (1yd) fusible web (eg Bondaweb)
½m (½yd) dark blue cotton fabric
20cm (8in) strip sand-coloured cotton fabric
1m (1yd) light-coloured fine cotton backing fabric
1m (1yd) lining fabric
Gold metallic machine thread
Other coloured metallic machine thread (optional)
Narrow ribbon (optional)
15cm (6in) embroidery hoop

Small and large gold star-shaped sequins
44cm (17½in) strip thin wood
46cm (18in) cotton tape 2.5cm (1in) wide
Tracing paper and thin card for templates

PREPARING THE KINGS

(Leave the faces, which are machine embroidered, until later.)

Trace all other parts from the patterns through onto the smooth side of a piece of fusible web. Leave space round each shape and immediately mark with a colour code and number to differentiate the kings. When you cut out the fusible web shapes, do not cut along the drawn line but leave a little space round each.

Iron the shapes onto the correct coloured fabric taking the grain lines into account. Cut out the shapes along the drawn line.

MAKING THE KINGS

Trace the outlines of the three kings and make templates (see Techniques and Stitches, p143). Do not include the 'gifts' at this stage.

Cut a rectangle each of backing fabric and fusible web 27 x 50cm (11 x 20in) and fuse the two together (see manufacturer's instructions).

Reverse the templates and draw round each on the backing fabric.

Peel the backing paper from the fused shapes and iron them carefully in position onto the backing fabric, using the patterns for the kings as a guide.

PREPARING THE HEADS

Draw the reverse image of the 3 heads onto tracing paper.

Pin the paper onto a square of brown cotton fabric and place in an embroidery hoop ready for free machine embroidery (see Techniques and Stitches, p140).

Using gold machine thread, and a straight stitch, work simple outlines over the tracing paper. Machine a few simple guide-lines for the beards and hair. (Leave the eyes, which can be hand-embroidered later.) Tear away the tracing paper. Work more details into the hair and beards. A small zigzag stitch couched over the straight lines gives more prominence.

Take the work out of the hoop and trim off all threads. Iron a piece of fusible web to the back of the heads and cut them out just outside the stitching lines.

Peel off the backing paper and iron them into position.

Cut out each king carefully.

PREPARING THE BACKGROUND

Cut a rectangle of backing fabric 63 x 48cm (25 x 19in). Measure down from the top edge 46cm (18in). Draw and baste a placement line for the 'sand'.

Cut a rectangle of blue fabric 47 x 48cm (18½ x 19in) and place on the backing fabric, pinning the 2 top edges together.

Baste the 2 layers again along the placement line from the back.

Cut a strip of sand-coloured fabric 19 x 48cm (7½ x 19in). Fold over a 12mm (½in) turning on a long edge, and pin and hem to the blue background along the placement line.

Baste all round the edge of the hanging and press well.

COMPLETING THE KINGS

Arrange the three kings on the background in a pleasing pattern. The second king can be brought forward and allowed to slightly overlap the first and third king.

Peel the backing paper from the first king and iron onto the background.

Set the machine up for ordinary sewing. Use a coloured metallic thread and decorate the skirt and cuff bands with rows of straight and zigzag stitch.

Change to gold thread and, using a small zigzag, work round all edges (excluding the face). Machine across intersections where one fabric meets another.

Decorate the crown with some small gold sequins.

Repeat for the other two kings. Decorate the skirts and sleeves with rows of stitching or bands of narrow ribbon. Sew small sequins to the skirt of the third king (see Techniques and Stitches, p138).

Prepare the gifts and position them on the hands using fusible web and zigzag stitch.

Embroider the eyes and eyebrows with a few hand stitches.

COMPLETING THE HANGING

Sew some large and small star sequins onto the background. Cut a piece of lining the same size as the hanging and, with right sides together, pin the lining onto the background. Machine round the edge leaving a 12mm (½in) seam allowance. Leave a gap of about 13cm (5in) along the bottom edge for turning. Trim the corners of the seam allowance. Turn right side out and press. Slip stitch the opening.

Cut a piece of tape 46cm (18in) and turn the ends under so that they are just shorter than the width of the hanging. Hand-stitch the long edges of the tape along the top of the hanging, leaving the ends open for the thin strip of wood.

Make a twisted cord (see Techniques and Stitches, p143) 56cm (22in) long and attach it securely to the top corners of the hanging.

Cut a thin strip of wood slightly shorter than the width of the hanging and slip it into the tape. Alternatively, mount the hanging over a board to give a flatter appearance.

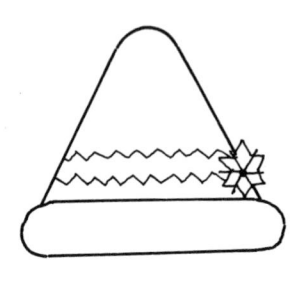 

Detail of decorated crowns

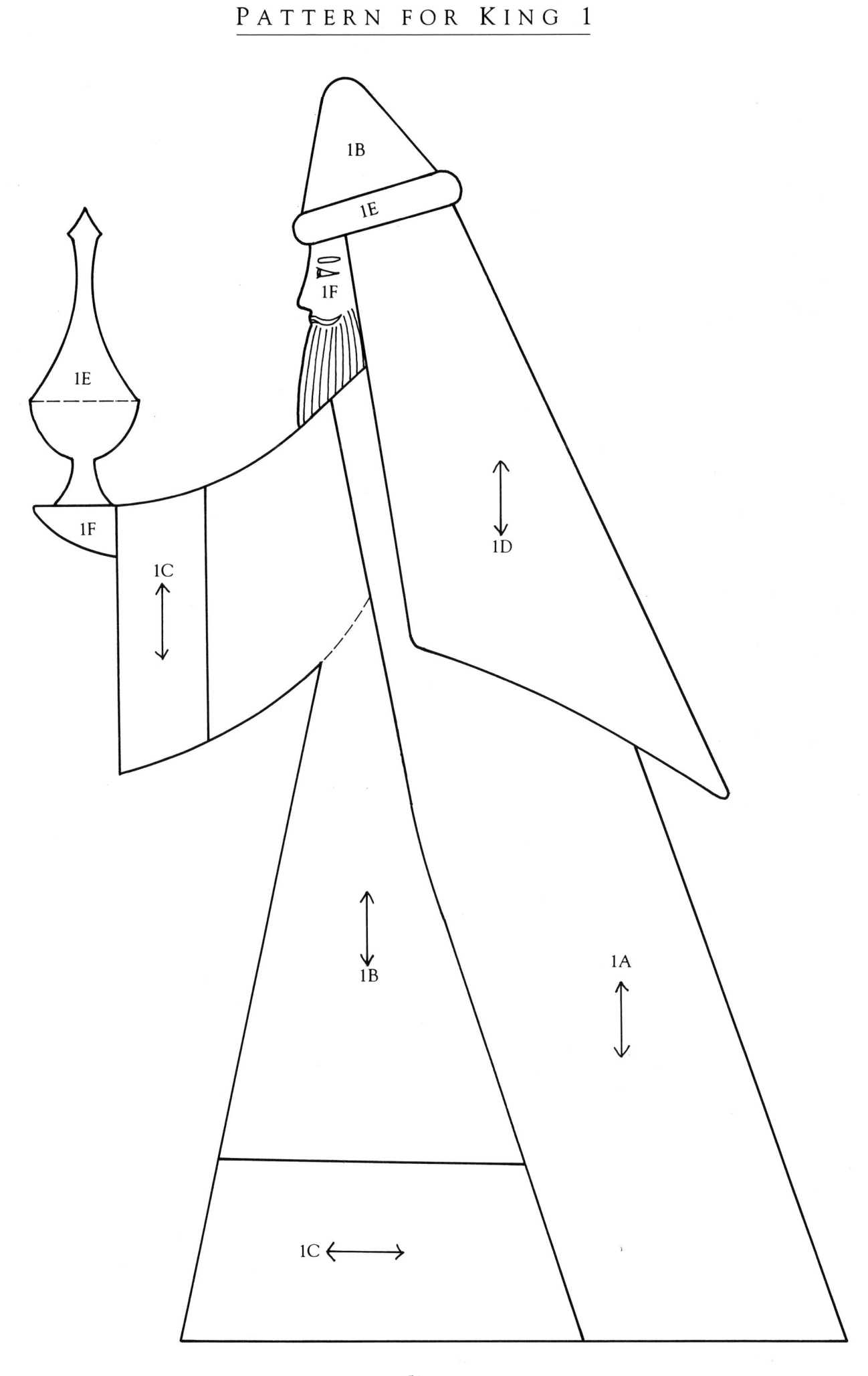

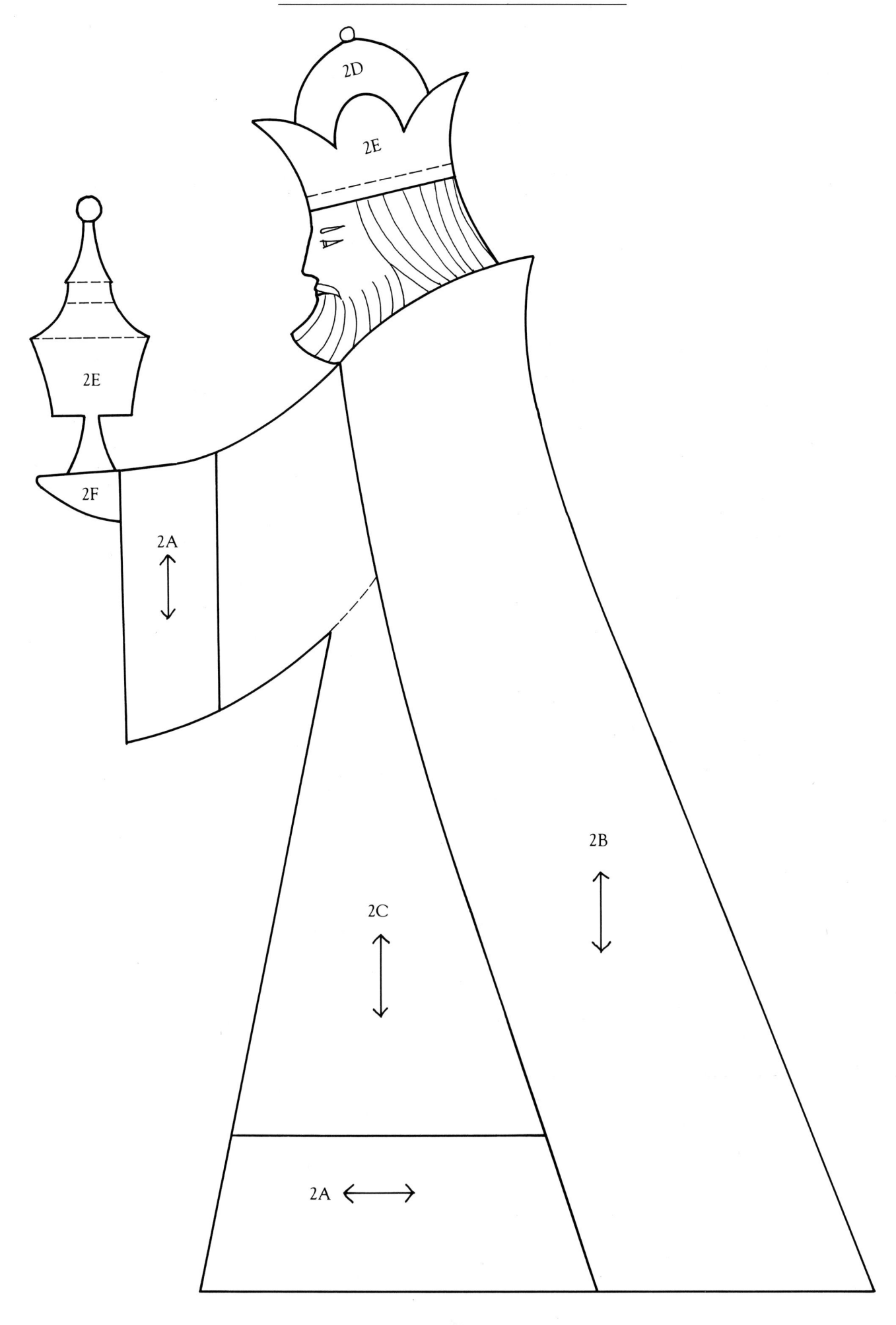

CARDHOLDER

The cardholder is an attractive way to display Christmas cards. It is made of two layers of fabric-covered card in three sections which are hinged for easy storage. A band of automatic decorative machine-stitching runs down the centre front of the cardholder.

•

APPROXIMATE SIZE

124 x 15cm (49 x 6in)

•

MATERIALS

46 x 76cm (18 x 30in) stiff card

70 x 122cm (27 x 48in) natural cotton or fine linen fabric

Green and red machine thread

PVA adhesive

Double-sided adhesive tape (optional)

Natural crochet cotton for hanging loop

2 curtain rings approximately 2.5cm (1in) in diameter

25cm (10in) of 12mm (½in) wide tape

43 x 38cm (17 x 15in) felt or thick paper for neatening back of cardholder

Red wool or yarn for tassel

CUTTING THE CARD

Use a cutting-board and craft knife and cut against a metal safety ruler. Measure and cut accurately, making sure that the corners are right angles.

For the front of the cardholder, cut 2 pieces of card 38 x 9cm (15 x 3½in) and 1 piece 46 x 9cm (18 x 3½in).

For the back of the cardholder, cut 2 pieces of card 38 x 15cm (15 x 6in) and 1 piece 46 x 15cm (18 x 6in).

Cut the 2 long pieces of card at one end to form a point. On the wider piece of card (cardholder back), mark the centre of one short side (A). Measure 7.5cm (3in) up from the corners (B) and join AB (Fig 1). Cut off the corners. Cut a point on the narrow piece of card (cardholder front) to match.

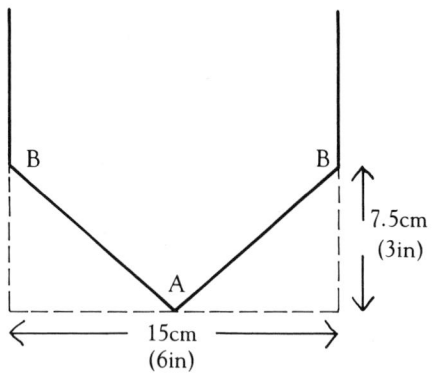

Fig 1 Showing the point at the base of the cardholder

CARDHOLDER FRONT

The centre front of the cardholder is decorated with a band of automatic machine stitching approximately 5cm (2in) wide using red and green machine thread. Experiment with varied rows of stitching on scraps of fabric to find an attractive combination.

The stitching is worked down the centre of fabric 18cm (7in) wide. You will need 1 piece 51cm (20in) long

and 2 pieces 43cm (17in) long.

If you are using up a long strip of fabric, it is a good idea to work the decorative band of stitching before cutting out the 3 sections. This will ensure that the rows match when the cardholder is assembled. Begin with the centre row and then work matching rows on each side. If you are using separate pieces of fabric, work each row on all pieces before you move on to the next row. Make sure that the rows are the same distance apart on each piece of fabric.

When covering the card with the decorated fabric, make sure that the stitching is in the centre of the card and that the rows are straight.

Stick a piece of double-sided adhesive tape down the centre front of a piece of card measuring 38 x 9cm (15 x 3½in). Place a piece of decorated fabric measuring 43 x 18cm (17 x 7in) right side down on a smooth surface. Place the card on the centre of the fabric. The sticky tape will hold it in place temporarily while you check to see if the stitching is straight. Adjust if necessary.

Spread a thin layer of adhesive all over the back of the card. Fold the fabric over the edges of the card and stick down. The fabric should meet in the centre back. Check again to make sure that the stitching is central and straight and the fabric is taut. Trim off the surplus fabric at the corners. The surface on the back of the card should be as smooth and as neat as possible.

Cover the other 2 pieces of narrow card in the same way, trimming the surplus fabric from behind the point on the longer piece.

CARDHOLDER BACK

Glue the fabric to the centre front of the card to ensure a good fixing when the cardholder is assembled.

Cut 2 pieces of fabric 43 x 20cm (17 x 8in) and 1 piece 51 x 20cm (20 x 8in). Lay the fabric right side

9mm (³⁄₈in)

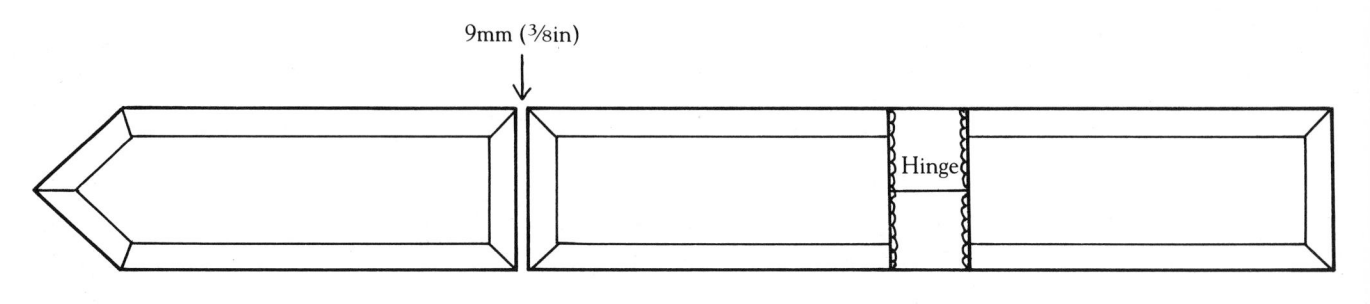

Fig 2 Back of cardholder showing one hinge in position

down on a smooth surface. Spread a 2.5cm (1in) band of adhesive down the middle of each piece of card and centre them on the fabric. There should be a border of fabric approximately 2.5cm (1in) wide all round the card. Smooth the fabric down and leave to dry.

Fold the fabric border over to the back of the card and glue down. Make sure the fabric is taut on the front of the card. Trim the surplus fabric from the corners and the point carefully. Leave to dry.

HINGES

Cut a piece of fabric 33 x 15cm (13 x 6in). Work a band of stitching down the centre to match the stitching on the front of the cardholder. Begin the first row in the middle of one long edge.

Fold the fabric with right sides facing and pin the short sides together to form a tube. Machine the seam leaving a 12mm (½in) seam allowance. Check that the tube is the same width as the cardholder back. Press the seam open. Turn to the right side and make sure that the decorative stitching is in the centre before it is pressed. Cut in half to make 2 hinges 15 x 7.5cm (6 x 3in). Zigzag along the raw edges, stitching through both layers of each hinge.

ASSEMBLING THE CARDHOLDER

Glue the back and front of the cardholder together down the centre only. The cards are tucked between the layers on each side.

Spread a 2.5cm (1in) band of adhesive down the centre of the right side of the back sections. Place the front sections on top, making sure that they are in the centre and the top and bottom edges match. Place books or magazines on top to make sure that the cardholder remains flat. Leave to dry.

Place all 3 sections face down on a flat surface with 9mm (³⁄₈in) spaces between them (Fig 2). Stick the hinges securely to the back of the cardholder, making sure that the centre of a hinge is over a space. Check that the hinges are straight and the rows of decorative stitching match. Leave to dry.

Fold a 12.5cm (5in) piece of tape 12mm (½in) wide through a curtain ring and stitch through both layers of tape close to the ring (Fig 3). Stick the ends of the tape together. Repeat for the other ring.

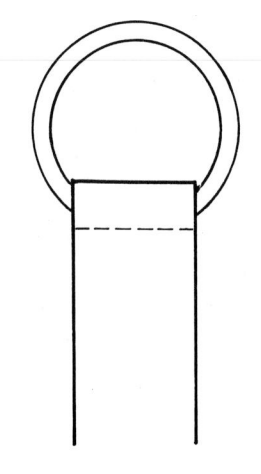

Fig 3 Showing the tape stitched to a curtain ring

Top edge

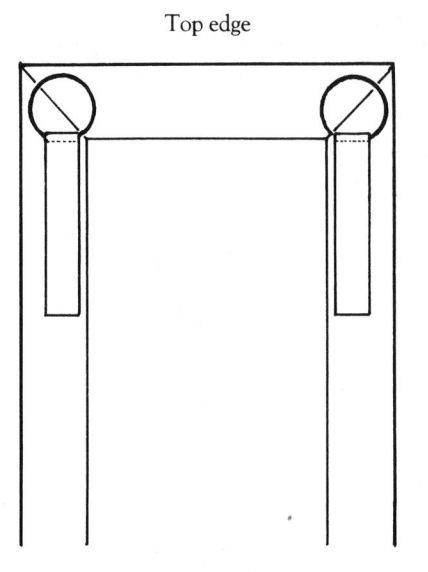

Fig 4 Back of cardholder showing the position of curtain rings

Stick the tapes securely to the top back of the cardholder (Fig 4).

Use natural crochet cotton to make a twisted cord 30cm (12in) long (see Techniques and Stitches, p143). Tie an end securely to each curtain ring to make a hanging loop.

Make a red tassel 15cm (6in) long (see Techniques and Stitches, p143). Stick the tying thread to the back of the cardholder so that the tassel hangs below the point.

Neaten the back of each section of the cardholder with felt or thick paper leaving a 12mm (½in) margin all round.

CROSS STITCH HANGING

Here is a chance to work some classic embroidery. Cross stitch is one of the oldest stitches and is a lovely way to create some traditional symbols of Christmas.

•

APPROXIMATE LENGTH

47cm (19in)

•

MATERIALS

20cm (¼yd) cream Aida cloth, 14 threads to 27mm (1in)

36 x 11cm (14 x 4½in) white non-woven pelmet stiffener (eg pelmet or craft quality Vilene)

Fusible web (eg Bondaweb) cut to the same size

20cm (¼yd) cream lining fabric

3 skeins red ⎫ stranded
3 skeins green ⎬ embroidery
Skein yellow ⎭ cotton

Fine tapestry needle

Squared pattern paper

15cm (6in) embroidery hoop

When using Aida fabric, follow the mesh of the coarse flat weave where holes are obvious. Each thread is actually made up of 4 fine threads in a group and stitches are worked from hole to hole.

The illustration given for the hanging is half size (Fig 1). Double the measurements and make a paper pattern. Pin this onto a piece of Aida cloth measuring 46 x 20cm (18 x 8in), making sure that the edge of the pattern follows the weave of the fabric. Baste round the pattern with a coloured thread. Remove the pattern.

Measure along the top edge and find the centre. Mark with a pin. Baste down the centre of the hanging from the pin with a coloured thread. This will help to position the embroidery.

PREPARING THE EMBROIDERY

Count 3 threads down the centre from the top edge of the hanging and mark with a pin. Begin the cross-stitch border in either direction below this point.

Use 2 strands of embroidery cotton and follow the charts for the cross-stitch panels.

Leave 3 threads between each of the 3 boxes.

Remember that all stitches must cross in the same direction (see Techniques and Stitches, p142).

MAKING THE HANGING

Pin the paper pattern onto the pelmet stiffener. Draw round it and cut out leaving 1cm (⅜in) allowance round the edge. Iron a piece of fusible web the same size onto the back of the pelmet stiffener (see manufacturer's instructions.

Cut out the panel along the drawn line. Peel away the backing paper from the fusible web. Position the panel exactly in place on the wrong side of the embroidered Aida and fuse together with a hot iron.

Trim away any surplus Aida fabric to leave 15cm (⅝in) turnings. Baste these to the back of the hanging. Press.

For the hanging loop make a twisted cord with 150cm (60in) of red stranded cotton (see Techniques and Stitches, p143). Stitch the cord in place at the back of the hanging.

Use the paper pattern and cut a piece of lining fabric leaving 15mm (⅝in) turnings. Pin to the back of the hanging, folding under the turnings all round.

Use a cream-coloured thread to slip stitch the lining to the hanging. Take out all basting threads.

Make a 9cm (3½in) tassel using green and red stranded cotton (see Techniques and Stitches, p143). Stitch to the point at the bottom and the hanging is complete.

EMBROIDERY CHART

⊡ Green

☑ Red

☑ Yellow

Details of candles on the tree (rays not shown) on chart

Fig 1 Half size pattern for hanging

ADVENT TREE

The Advent Tree becomes more and more colourful as Christmas approaches. Each day during Advent, children can hang a decoration from one of the red wooden beads. The large star is added to the top of the tree on Christmas day.

•

APPROXIMATE SIZE

91 x 76cm (36 x 30in)

•

MATERIALS

97 x 76cm (38 x 30in) dark green felt

25 x 20cm (10 x 8in) light green felt

60 x 92cm (24 x 36in) red felt

Machine thread: dark green, light green and red

97 x 76cm (38 x 30in) dark green cotton fabric

Tracing paper

Fusible web (eg Bondaweb)

25 red wooden beads approximately 1cm (³⁄₈in) in diameter

4 green wooden beads approximately 8mm (⁵⁄₁₆in) in diameter

16 small black beads for eyes

Red crochet cotton for hanging loops

76cm (30in) of 2.5cm (1in) wide dark green tape

74cm (29in) of 6mm (¼in) diameter dowel

MAKING THE TREE

Make a full-size pattern for the tree. The easiest way to do this is to trace the sides (AB and AC) of the reduced pattern and extend them until they measure 99cm (39in). Join BC. Add a 2.5cm (1in) border to the outside of the pattern by drawing a line all round, parallel to the edge of the pattern. Cut out the pattern on the outer line.

The tree is made from dark green felt strengthened with a backing of green cotton fabric. The 2 layers are fused together with fusible web.

Draw the pattern on the smooth (paper) side of the fusible web and iron onto the cotton backing. Cut out the tree and remove the paper backing. Iron onto the felt using a dry iron and damp cloth. Cut out the felt.

Using red machine thread, decorate the tree with bands of machine zigzag and straight stitching, about 2cm (¾in) wide. Experiment with different combinations on scraps of felt (Fig 1). The width of the bands varies slightly but the spaces between the bands are all 4.5cm (1¾in) wide. Work the bands parallel to the bottom edge of the tree. Begin the first band of stitching 4cm (1½in) up from the bottom edge. Stitch to the side edges in each row.

Cut the 2.5cm (1in) border off the pattern and draw round the pattern on the back of the tree. Cut out carefully. Zigzag round the edge twice using matching machine thread. Do not have the stitches too close together or the edge of the felt will stretch. Try a sample on a spare piece of felt.

Use red thread to sew on the red wooden beads. Space them evenly across the tree. Sew the first bead to the point at the top of the tree. Sew a row of 3 beads 20cm (8in) below. The rest of the beads are sewn on in rows of 5, 7 and 9 with the rows 18cm (7in) apart.

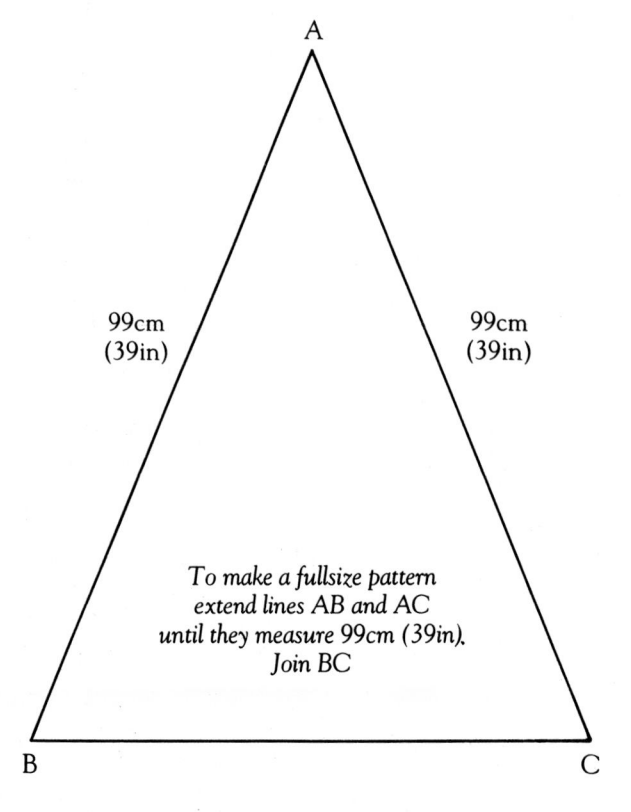

A

99cm (39in)   99cm (39in)

*To make a fullsize pattern
extend lines AB and AC
until they measure 99cm (39in).
Join BC*

B   C

Patterns for Advent Tree, Lovebird Tree and Lovebird Rope

STAR 1
STAR 2
STAR 3
HEART 1
HEART 2
HEART 3
BELL
WING
BIRD BODY
STOCKING

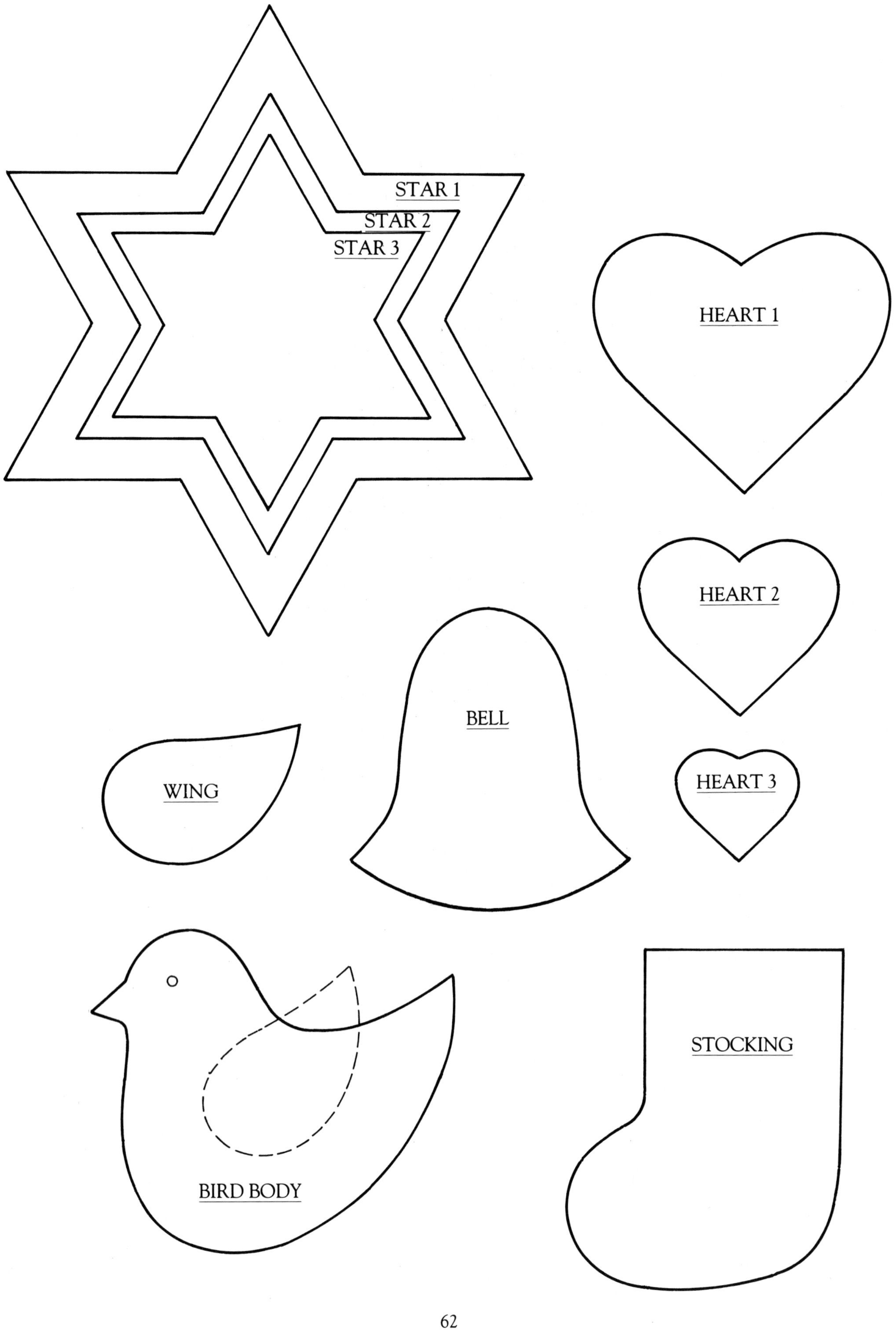

Using red crochet cotton, make a twisted cord about 13cm (5in) long (see Techniques and Stitches, p143). Sew the ends of the cord securely to the back of the tree behind the top point, to make a hanging loop.

Cut a 76cm (30in) piece of tape 2.5cm (1in) wide. Turn the ends under to neaten and stitch the long edges to the back of the tree close to the bottom edge. Leave the ends open for the dowel. Cut a piece of dowel 6mm (¼in) in diameter so that it is slightly shorter than the width of the tree and insert it into the channel made with the tape.

MAKING THE DECORATIONS

General instructions: trace the patterns and make templates (see Techniques and Stitches, p143) for the bird body and wing, bell, stocking, size 1 and 3 stars and size 1 heart. The hearts, stars, bells and bird bodies are all made in the same way from 4 layers of red felt.

Draw round the template on the smooth (paper) side of fusible web and iron onto red felt. Cut out the shape and remove the paper backing. The hanging loops can be added at this stage but care must be taken later when cutting out as it is easy to snip the loop by mistake.

Cut a 13cm (5in) piece of red crochet cotton and tie the ends together. Place the knotted ends under the cut-out shape so that the loop emerges in the correct place (see instructions for individual decorations). Fuse the shapes onto another piece of red felt using a dry iron and damp cloth. Place on top of 2 more layers of felt (4 layers in all).

Use matching machine thread to stitch all round the shape, working over the edge with a narrow zigzag stitch. Cut out carefully close to the stitching. Zigzag round the shape again with a wider stitch.

Birds Following the general instructions make 8 bird bodies from red felt and 16 wings from light green felt. Use only 2 layers of felt for the wings. Sew small black beads in place for the eyes. Slip stitch a wing to each side of the body. Add a short hanging loop to the top of the bird between the wings.

Stars Make 1 size 1 star and 4 size 3 stars, following the general instructions. Add a short hanging loop to a point on the small stars and the centre back on the large star.

Heart Make 4 size 1 hearts, following the general instructions. Add a short hanging loop to the centre top of the hearts.

Bells Make 4 bells, following the general instructions. Sew a green bead to the centre of the bottom edge of the bells. Add a short hanging loop to the centre top of the bells.

Stockings Make 4 stockings. To make 1 stocking you will need a piece of red felt approximately 9 x 13cm (3½ x 5in). Fold a 1cm (⅜in) hem on the long edge and press. With matching machine thread, work a row of narrow zigzag stitches over the edge of the hem. Place the template on the wrong side of the felt with the top edge against the fold. Draw round the template and cut out 1 stocking piece. Place the stocking on the other half of the felt, wrong sides together, with the folded edges matching. Zigzag round the stocking with a narrow stitch, leaving the folded edge open. Cut out the stocking and zigzag round again using a slightly wider stitch. Add a short hanging loop to the top of the back seam.

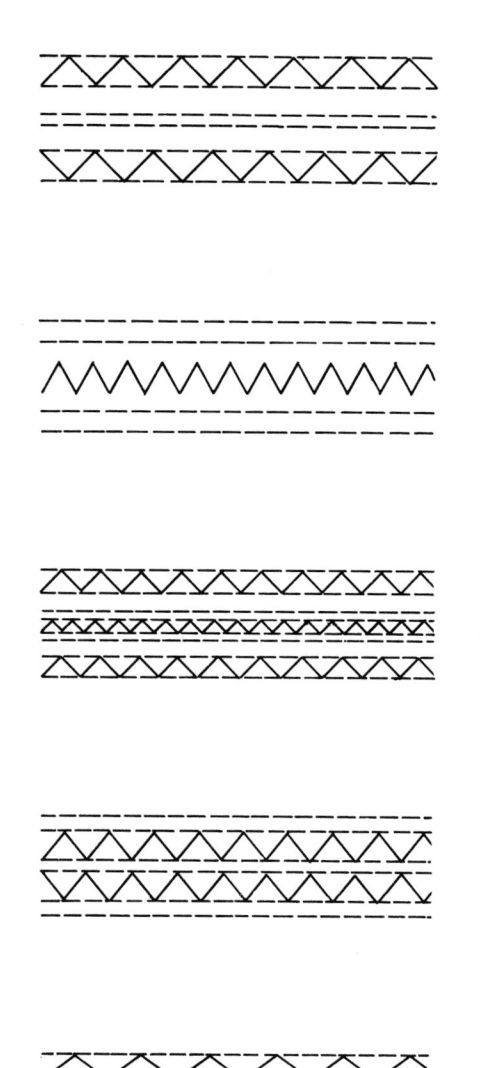

Fig 1 Decorative bands of machine zigzag and straight stitch

LOVEBIRD TREE

The Lovebird Tree is an attractive alternative to the Advent Tree (see p60). The birds, hearts and star are made in the same way and slip stitched to the background.

•

APPROXIMATE SIZE

74 x 23cm (29 x 9in)

•

MATERIALS

76 x 25cm (30 x 10in) natural furnishing fabric

Matching lining fabric and machine thread

51 x 61cm (20 x 24in) red felt and matching machine thread

20 x 10cm (8 x 4in) light green felt and matching machine thread

56 x 2.5cm (22 x 1in) mid-green felt and matching machine thread

6 small black beads (eyes)

Red crochet cotton for hanging loop

46cm (18in) of 6mm (¼in) diameter dowel

Fusible web (eg Bondaweb)

50cm (20in) of 1.5cm (⅝in) wide cream tape

Tracing paper and thin card for templates

MAKING THE BIRDS, HEARTS AND STAR

Trace the patterns for the bird, the size 2 star and the size 2 and 3 hearts (see Advent Tree, p62) and make templates (see Techniques and Stitches, p143).

Following the instructions for the Advent Tree, p63, make 3 size 2 hearts and 1 size 2 star. Make 3 pairs of birds, sewing the eyes and wings to 1 side only.

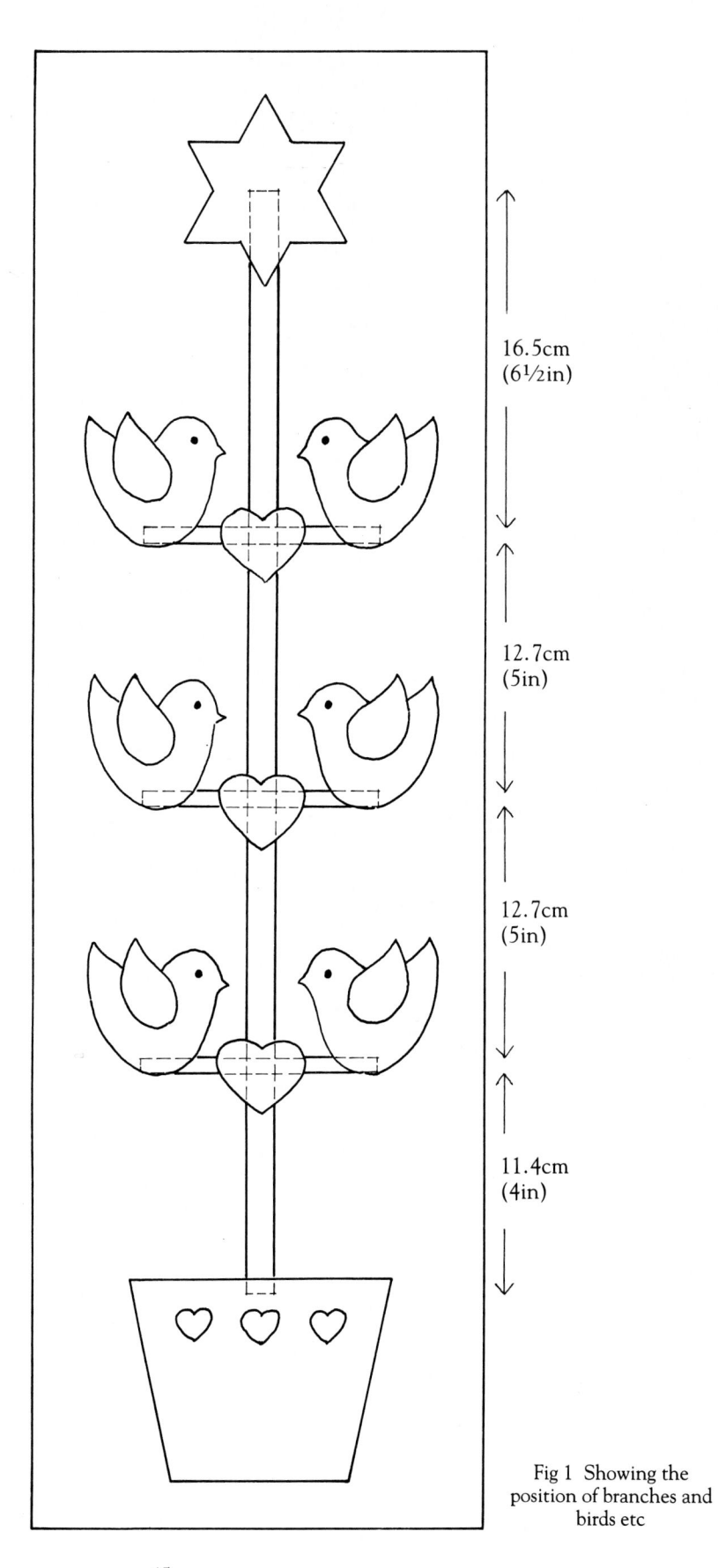

16.5cm (6½in)

12.7cm (5in)

12.7cm (5in)

11.4cm (4in)

Fig 1 Showing the position of branches and birds etc

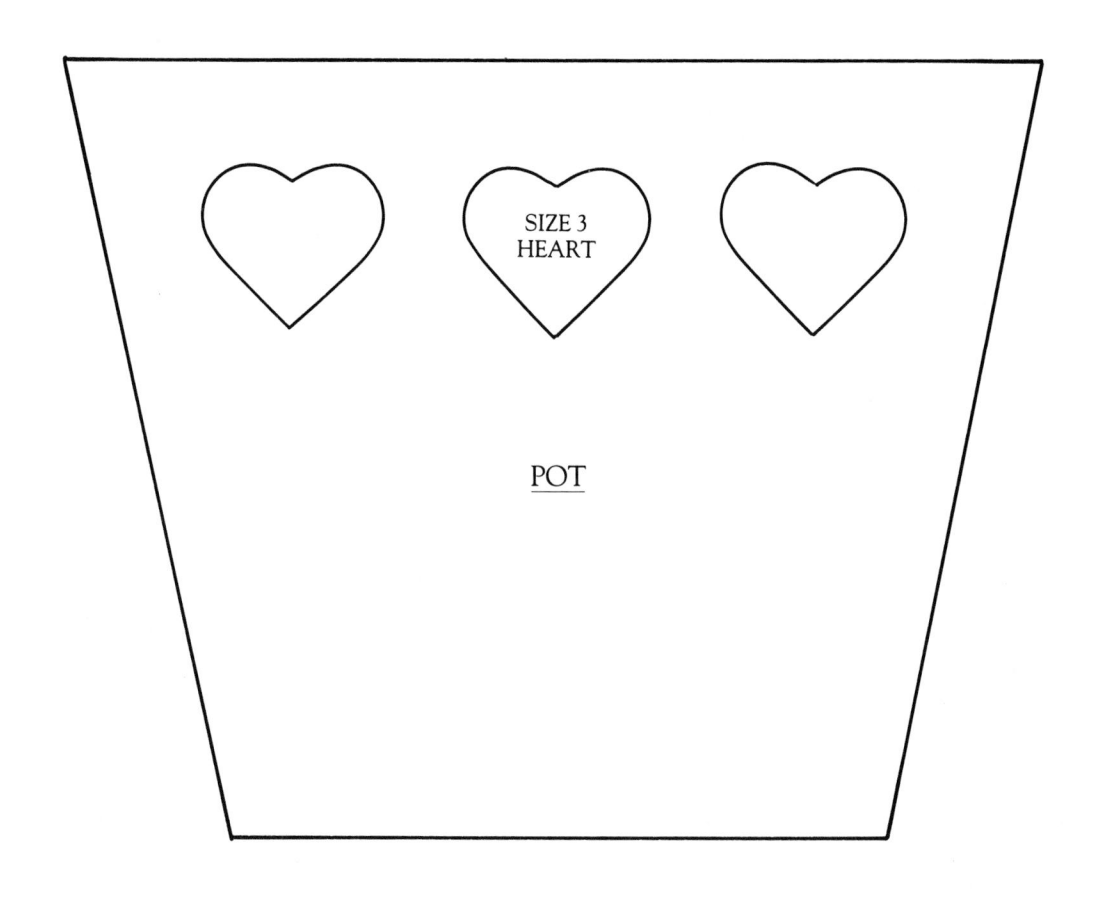

MAKING THE BACKGROUND

Cut a piece of natural furnishing fabric (background) and a piece of matching lining fabric 76 x 25cm (30 x 10in).

Fusible web is used to fuse the trunk, branches and pot to the background. Machine zigzag, using matching machine thread, is then worked over the edges of the shapes. Draw the trunk and branches (see below) and trace the pot pattern onto the smooth (paper) side of the fusible web and iron onto the appropriate coloured felt. Cut out the felt and fuse in place using a dry iron and damp cloth.

The trunk is a strip of mid-green felt measuring 56 x 1.5cm (22 x ⅝in). Fuse to the centre of the background with the top of the trunk 8cm (3in) down from the top edge of the background. With matching thread, machine down both sides of the trunk with a narrow zigzag stitch.

Cut 3 strips of mid-green felt 13cm x 6mm (5 x ¼in) for the branches. Fuse to the background in the positions shown in Fig 1. The branches should

be at right angles to the trunk. Make sure that the centres of the branches are placed on the centre of the trunk. Zigzag along the branches with matching machine thread.

Fuse the pot onto another piece of red felt. Machine all round over the edge of the pot with a narrow zigzag stitch, using matching thread. Cut the second piece of felt close to the stitching.

Fuse 3 light green size 3 hearts to the pot in the positions shown on the pot pattern. Carefully machine all round over the edges of the hearts with a narrow zigzag stitch, using matching machine thread. Iron a piece of fusible web onto the back of the pot. Remove paper backing and place the centre of the pot over the base of the trunk in the position shown in Fig 1. Make sure the top edge of the pot is at right angles to the trunk. Fuse the pot to the background. Zigzag all round over the edge of the pot with matching machine thread using a wider stitch.

With right sides together, pin the lining to the background. Machine

round the edge leaving a 12mm (½in) seam allowance. Leave a gap of about 13cm (5in) in the bottom edge for turning. Trim the corners of the seam allowance. Turn to the right side and press. Slip stitch the opening.

Cut 2 pieces of tape 25cm (10in) long and turn the ends under so that they are just a little shorter than the width of the hanging. Hand stitch the long edges of the tape to the lining at the top and bottom of the hanging. Leave the ends open for the dowel.

Slip stitch the birds, star and hearts to the background. Place a pair of birds (no wings or eyes at the back) on each branch so that the bases of the birds just cover the ends of the branch. Centre the star over the top of the trunk and a heart between each pair of birds (see Fig 1).

Make a twisted cord about 28cm (11in) long (see Techniques and Stitches, p143) and attach it securely to the top corners of the hanging.

Cut 2 pieces of dowel slightly shorter than the width of the hanging and insert them into the tape at the top and bottom of the hanging.

LOVEBIRD ROPE

Made from bright red and green felt, the lovebird rope is a very cheerful addition to the decorations at Christmas. Use other brightly coloured felts to make a bird rope to decorate a child's nursery or bedroom all the year round.

.

APPROXIMATE LENGTH

48cm (19in)

.

MATERIALS

40 x 30cm (16 x 12in) red felt

Matching machine thread

20 x 10cm (8 x 4in) light green felt

Matching machine thread

33 red wooden beads approximately 6mm (¼in) in diameter

1 red wooden bead approximately 1cm (⅜in) in diameter

6 small black beads (eyes)

Approximately 36cm (14in) narrow red ribbon

Strong red thread (button thread)

Fusible web (eg Bondaweb)

Tracing paper and thin card for templates

MAKING THE BIRDS AND HEARTS

Trace the bird patterns and the size 2 heart pattern (see Advent Tree, p62) and make templates (see Techniques and Stitches, p143).

Make 3 birds and 5 size 2 hearts, following the instructions for the Advent Tree.

ASSEMBLING THE ROPE

Begin assembling the rope at the bottom. Cut a piece of strong red thread about 120cm (48in) long. With 1 small red wooden bead on the thread to act as a stopper, thread both ends through a long needle and start

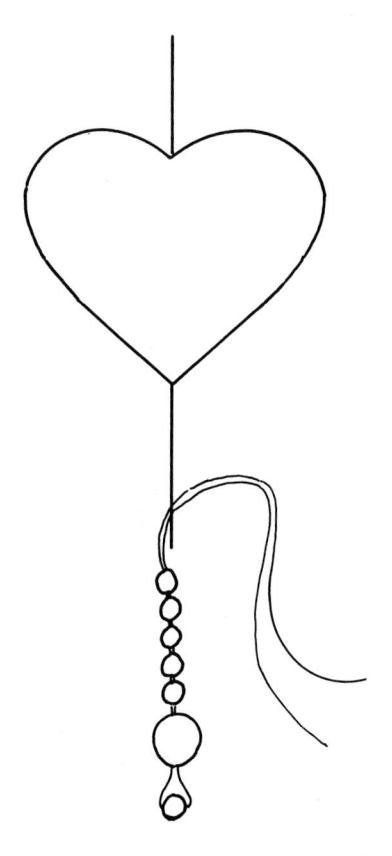

Fig 1 Stringing the rope starting at the bottom

Fig 2 Showing the positions of birds, hearts and beads

67

by stringing the large bead and then 5 small beads (Fig 1). Take the needle through the centre of a heart, making sure that the needle does not go through to the back.

Continue stringing beads, hearts and birds in the order shown in Fig 2. Take the needle through the birds in the position shown in Fig 3, again making sure that the needle does not go through to the back.

When the stringing is complete, fasten off the ends of the thread very securely behind the wings of the top bird. The rope should hang easily. If the threads are pulled too tight when fastening off, the rope will be distorted.

Cut a piece of narrow red ribbon 36cm (14in) long for the hanging loop. Turn under 6mm (¼in) at each end to neaten. Stitch one end to each side of the top bird behind the wings.

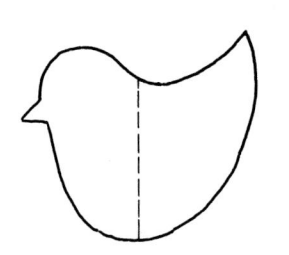

Fig 3 Showing the position of the thread

BIRD ROPE

This hanging with its Eastern influence is not difficult to make and looks very festive when made in seasonal fabrics.

•

APPROXIMATE LENGTH

71cm (28in)

•

MATERIALS

20cm (8in) various seasonal cotton fabrics

10 large beads

1 bell (optional – a tassel will do)

Sequins

PVA adhesive

Polyester stuffing

Tracing paper and thin card for templates

The rope in the photograph has 9 birds but you may have fewer

Trace the patterns for the body and tail and make templates (see Techniques and Stitches, p143).

Draw round the templates on the wrong side of the fabric and cut out a pair of body pieces and a pair of tail pieces for each bird, reversing the templates as necessary, and adding a 6mm (¼in) seam allowance.

PATTERN FOR BIRD ROPE

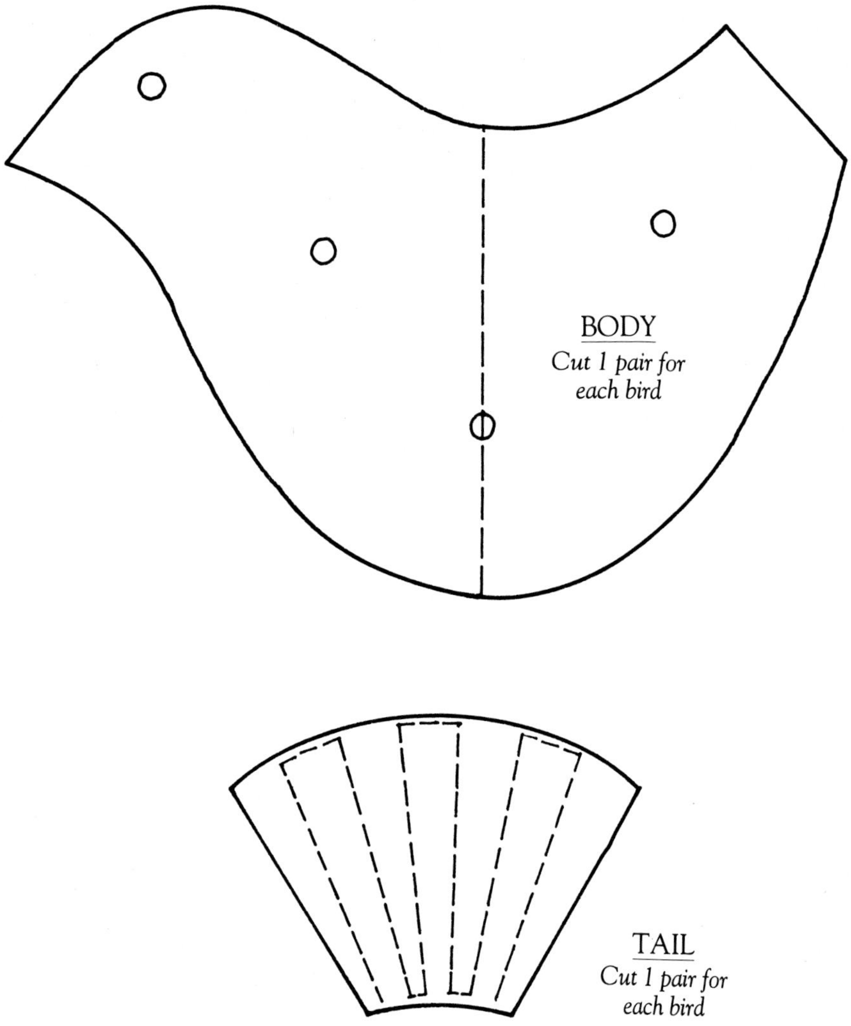

BODY
Cut 1 pair for each bird

TAIL
Cut 1 pair for each bird

MAKING A BIRD

At the tail end of the 2 body pieces, turn down a 6mm (¼in) turning towards the wrong side and press. (This will be the opening for the stuffing and where the tail will be inserted.)

With right sides together, pin the 2 pieces so that the marked lines match. Place the pins across the seam so that you can machine over them.

Use a small stitch and machine round the bird along the marked line (working gently over the pins), starting and finishing at the tail opening. It is a good idea to work backwards over the stitches for a short distance at the start and finish to secure the threads.

Trim the seam allowance to about 3mm (⅛in). Also trim the fabric away from the point of the beak.

Turn the bird right side out and stuff at the tail opening with small pieces of polyester stuffing. The bird looks more attractive if it is not over-stuffed.

```
┌─────────────────────────────────┐
│ ┌─ ─ ─ ─ ─ ─ ─ ─ ─ ─ ─ ─ ─ ─ ─┐ │ ┤ 2cm (¾in)
│ └─ ─ ─ ─ ─ ─ ─ ─ ─ ─ ─ ─ ─ ─ ─┘ │
└─────────────────────────────────┘
```
18cm (7in)

Fig 1 Strip for hanging loop showing fold lines (not to scale)

Decorate both sides with a few sequins (see Techniques and Stitches, p138), including one for the eye.

MAKING THE TAIL

With right sides together, pin the 2 tail pieces and stitch round 3 sides, leaving the base open. Secure the threads, trim the seam allowance and turn the tail right side out.

Insert a little stuffing and machine quilt using the pattern as a guide.

Insert the tail into the bird, pin and slip stitch in place.

MAKING UP THE ROPE

Take a strong thread approximately 152cm (60in) long and tie a bell at the centre point, then bring both ends together and thread onto a long needle.

Pass the needle through a bead and then through a bird, using the dotted line on the pattern as a guide. Continue to thread birds and beads alternately, finishing with a bead. Leave the thread in the needle.

Make a hanging loop from one of the seasonal fabrics.

Cut a rectangle 18 x 2cm (7 x ¾in) (Fig 1).

Fold in the short ends to the wrong side.

Fold in the long ends to the wrong side.

Fold again down the centre. Press.

Slip stitch the folded edges together to make a narrow strip. Bring the ends together and stitch. Fasten off.

Now attach the stringing threads to the loop securely, fasten off and the rope is complete.

BIRD TREE HANGING

The little felt birds on this tree, which look as if they are about to fly away, have wires running through them, and these are then glued behind two pieces of fabric-covered card.

·

LENGTH

19cm (7¾in)

·

MATERIALS

30cm (12in) green seasonal cotton fabric

20cm (¼yd) each red and dark green felt

12 gold star sequins

Red and green embroidery thread

Craft wire

Wire-cutters

6 small red beads (they must be large enough to thread onto the wire)

Polyester stuffing

25cm (10in) narrow red ribbon

PVA adhesive

Thin card

Tracing paper and thin card for templates

Clothes pegs to assist the fixing of the adhesive

Trace the patterns of the bird and wing and make templates (see Techniques and Stitches, p143).

For the 6 birds, use the templates and cut out 12 bird pieces from the red felt and 12 wings from the green felt.

PREPARING THE WINGS

Sew a sequin with red embroidery thread onto each wing to make 6 pairs (Fig 1) (see Techniques and Stitches, p138).

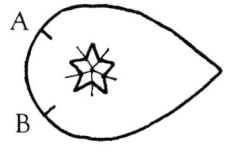

Fig 1 Wing decorated with a sequin

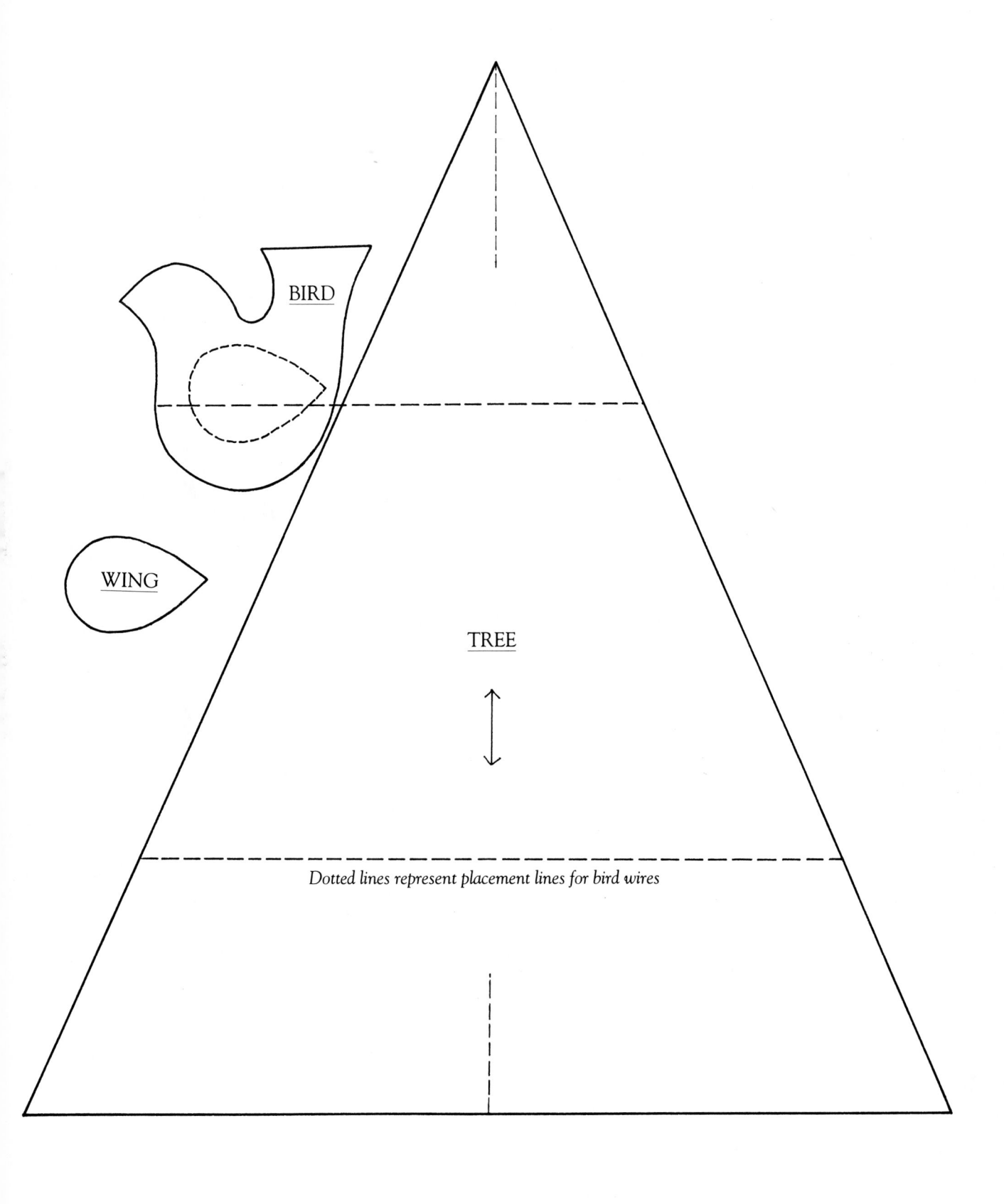

BIRD

WING

TREE

Dotted lines represent placement lines for bird wires

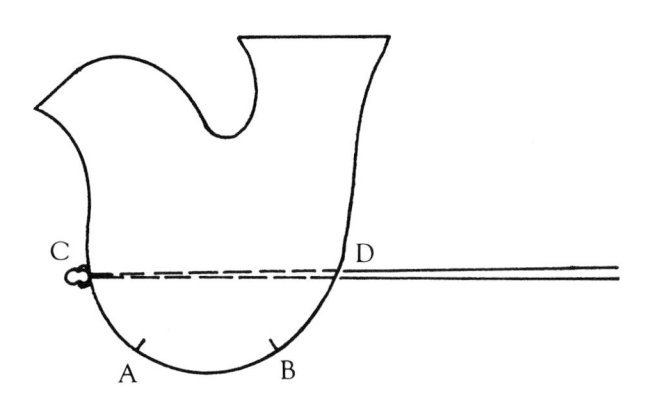

Fig 2 Showing a bead twisted onto a wire

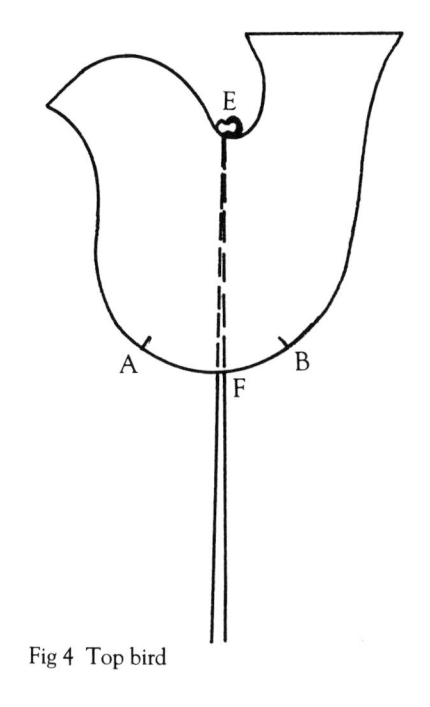

Fig 3 Side bird

Fig 4 Top bird

Blanket stitch (see Techniques and Stitches, p142) the edge of each, starting at point A round the wing to point B and finish by blanket stitching it to a bird section through to A.

PREPARING THE BIRDS

The top and side birds are fixed in place by wires inserted through them, and these are then glued in place between 2 pieces of card.

First prepare the wires. Cut 5 lengths measuring 14cm (5½in). Thread a bead onto the centre of each, fold the wire in two and give a twist to the bead to hold it firmly onto the wire (Fig 2).

THE FOUR SIDE BIRDS

Take 2 pairs of red bird pieces and blanket stitch them together round the edge with green embroidery thread, starting at point A. Work up the breast, insert a wire at C to come out at point D (Fig 3).

Continue round the bird, blanket stitching over the wire at D, to point B. Insert a little polyester stuffing into the bird (just enough to puff it out a little) and complete the stitching across the gap.

THE TOP BIRD

This is constructed in the same way, but insert the wire at E to come out at point F (Fig 4).

THE HANGING BIRD

The bird at the bottom has no wire but instead is hung by a thread from the bottom of the tree. Make it in the same way and attach a green thread 6cm (2¼in) to the bird at point E.

COMPLETING THE HANGING

Trace the triangular tree pattern and make a template. Use this to cut 2 pieces of thin card.

Now cut 2 pieces of green fabric, using the template, leaving 1cm (⅜in) turnings.

Glue all turnings down over the back of the cards. (Don't glue the front of the cards.) Cut away any surplus fabric from the corners as you glue.

Take 1 triangle and on the wrong side mark the placement lines for the wires on the card as shown on the pattern.

Position the birds in place and glue the wires down along the placement lines.

Glue the hanging thread of the bottom bird along its placement line. Leave the adhesive to dry thoroughly. Glue all over the back of the second triangle and place over the first, being very exact about matching the corners. Clip clothes pegs round the edge of the triangles to add pressure while the glue dries.

Make a hanging loop with red ribbon and attach it to the bead of the topmost bird, and the hanging is complete.

SNOWFLAKE MOBILE

These delicate snowflakes are hung together on a ring to make a beautiful mobile. They are machine embroidered on cotton organdie with lacy fillings in their centres. Individual snowflakes can be made for the Christmas tree or to hang at a window.

·

APPROXIMATE LENGTH

50cm (20in)

·

MATERIALS

½m (½yd) white cotton organdie

½m (½yd) medium-weight iron-on fabric stiffener (eg Vilene)

½m (½yd) white nylon net

White machine embroidery thread

12cm (5in) embroidery hoop

Sharp pencil

Tracing paper

Piece of polystyrene (often used in packaging)

OR a board which will take pins easily (macramé board)

Plastic bag

Spray starch

20cm (8in) diameter metal lampshade ring

White fluffy knitting yarn

Silver crochet thread

6 x 5mm (³/₁₆in) silver beads

1 x 1cm (³/₈in) silver bead

Fine silver thread

PVA adhesive

MAKING A SNOWFLAKE

Using a sharp pencil, make a tracing of a snowflake from one of the patterns provided.

Iron the fabric stiffener onto the organdie. Cut a piece 18cm (7in) square. Cut a square of net the same size and place behind the organdie.

Pin the tracing onto the organdie and place the 2 layers into an embroidery hoop. (You may prefer to work several snowflakes at one time in a larger hoop.)

Set your machine for free machine embroidery (see Techniques and Stitches, p140).

Use a straight stitch and outline the simplest details of the snowflake, working over the tracing. Leave details until later.

Take the work out of the hoop and tear away the paper from the stitching. Tweezers will help this task.

Now with sharp pointed scissors, cut away the unwanted areas (see patterns). In some areas you may like to cut away the organdie only, revealing the net below.

COMPLETING THE SNOWFLAKE

Put the work back in the hoop to complete the embroidery.

Use a straight stitch and machine down the centre of the bars, working across the cut area in the middle. Keep the stitching going in a continuous line, working back over the stitched lines where necessary.

Complete the lace filling where applicable (Figs 1a and 1b) (see Techniques and Stitches, p141, for lace filling).

Set your machine to zigzag. Choose a narrow stitch width and work over some of the decorative stitching on the bars to give a stronger effect.

Zigzag round the edge of the snowflake and round the cut work areas.

Fig 1a

Fig 1b Showing lace filling

Finally, take the work out of the hoop and very carefully cut out the snowflake close to the zigzagged outline.

Cover a piece of polystyrene with a plastic bag to make a blocking board. Pin the snowflakes onto this and spray with starch to stiffen. Leave to dry.

The mobile in the photograph has 9 snowflakes – 5 large and 4 small ones.

Attach a good length of fine silver thread to each snowflake at the end of a bar.

PREPARING THE HANGING RING

The ring is wrapped with knitting yarn. To start wrapping, put a dab of adhesive on the ring. Lay a few centimetres of yarn along this and begin wrapping back over it (Fig 2). Continue wrapping round the ring and finish off by firmly binding the yarn with sewing cotton.

Cut off the yarn close to the binding.

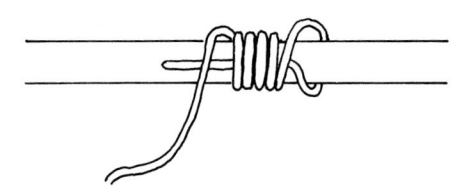

Fig 2 Showing how to begin wrapping a thread along the ring

the photograph is wooden and painted silver.)

It is necessary to hang the mobile at this stage in order to position the snowflakes. (A garden cane strung across and tied to the backs of two chairs will do.)

ASSEMBLING THE MOBILE

The assembly of the mobile is left somewhat to the reader's discretion.

Alternate small and large snowflakes round the ring, and make each hang at a different level. The aim is to give the impression of snowflakes falling from a wintery sky.

A good tip is to loop a snowflake over a bead and fix temporarily with a little adhesive tape. Repeat with the other flakes until you find attractive levels for all of them. Take each off its bead, tie a loop and cut off any surplus thread.

The mobile illustrated in the photograph has 3 extra snowflakes hanging down the centre of the ring. These are strung one below the other a few centimetres apart and threaded through the knot at the top. The hanging thread is fixed in the knot with the aid of a needle.

The knotted crochet threads can be tied again above the bead to make a hanging loop.

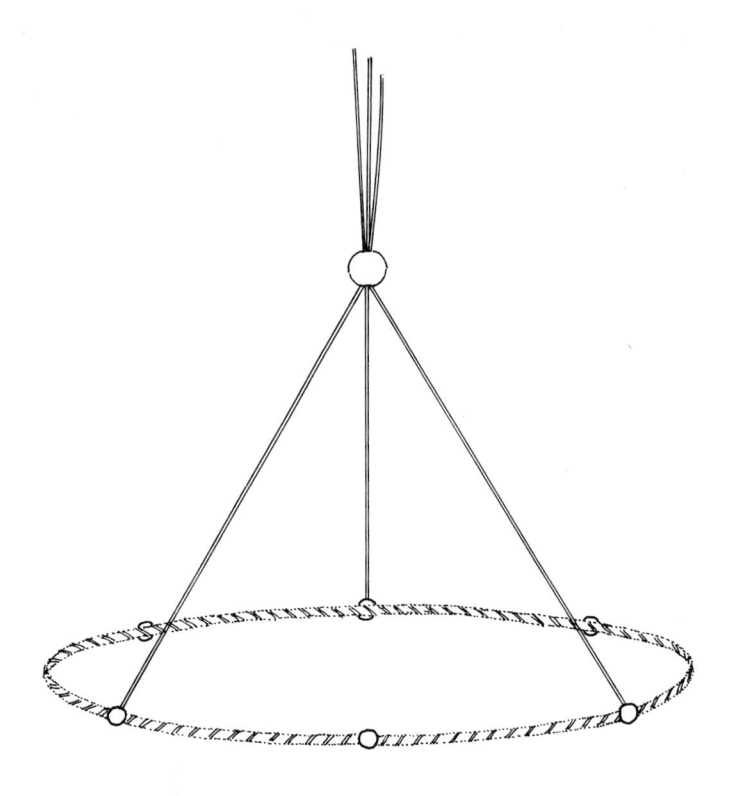

Fig 3 Showing the completed hanging ring

Now wrap the ring again with silver crochet thread, leaving gaps for the white yarn to show through.

Divide the ring into 6 equal parts and sew a bead at each point. Position them on the outer side of the ring; the snowflakes will hang from these (Fig 3).

Tie 3 lengths of silver crochet thread, approximately 50cm (20in), onto the ring at each alternate point. Bring them together and knot 18cm (7in) along the threads.

String a bead onto the threads and pull down over the knot. (The bead needs to have a large hole. The one in

HEART MOBILE

This pretty little mobile with a Scandinavian influence is extremely easy to make and requires only a little machine stitchery for its construction. The hearts are made of pelmet Vilene and are strung together in groups of six round a hoop.

APPROXIMATE LENGTH

44cm (17in)

•

MATERIALS

30cm (12in) white non-woven pelmet stiffener (eg pelmet or craft quality Vilene)

The inner ring of an embroidery hoop 20cm (8in)

6 x 5mm (³/₁₆in) natural wooden beads

1 x 1cm (³/₈in) red bead

Red machine thread

Red crochet cotton or string

PVA adhesive

Tea-bag

Red dye

Tracing paper and thin card for templates

MAKING THE HEARTS

Begin by cutting the pelmet stiffener into half, one half for the cream hearts and the other for the red. Take one half and cut it into smaller pieces. Dip the pieces for 5 minutes into a solution of cold tea made from a tea-bag.

Cut the other half into manageable pieces (keep them flat in the dye bath). Use a purchased red dye and follow the manufacturer's instructions.

Trace each heart and make · templates (see Techniques and Stitches, p143).

Draw round the templates and cut out the required number of hearts.

Decorate the 6 cream hearts with a row of red zigzag stitches.

Make 6 tracings of the assembly guide.

A row of 6 hearts is machined down onto each tracing using red machine thread. Pull plenty of thread from the machine before you start as this is used for the hanging loop.

Don't pin the hearts to the paper, just hold them in place on the tracing and machine through the centre of each. When you reach the bottom heart, machine back up a short distance to fix the threads.   Repeat this operation to make 6 hangings.

Tear away the backing paper.

Make a hanging loop at the top of each row of hearts by knotting the machine threads.

ASSEMBLING THE MOBILE

Divide the hanging ring into 6 equal parts, by making 6 marks and gluing a bead onto the inside at each point.

At each alternate point tie a strong red hanging thread 50cm (20in) long onto the ring. Check that the ring hangs correctly, then bring the 3 threads together and knot 15cm (6in) along the threads.

Thread a red bead onto these threads and pull down over the knot. Knot the threads again above the bead to make a hanging loop.

Cut out 6 more red hearts using the template indicated by a * on the pattern and glue each heart to the front of the ring at the hanging points.

Hang the hearts onto the beads and the mobile is complete.

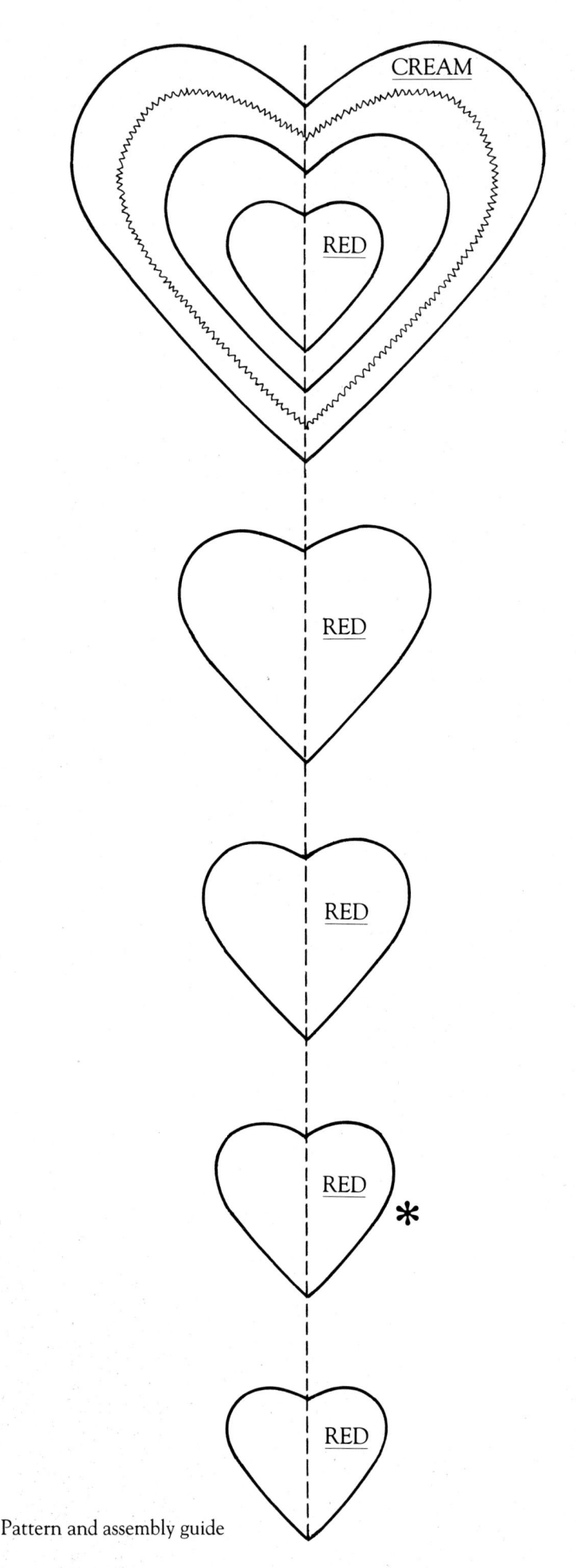

Pattern and assembly guide

Christmas
Cards

ROSE WINDOW CARD

The dramatic effect of stained glass is achieved with small pieces of richly coloured fabrics held in place on a backing fabric with simple free machine stitchery. This is then mounted behind a fretted card.

•

•

MATERIALS

Scraps of different coloured and textured fabrics

24cm (9½in) square fine cotton backing fabric

Variegated metallic machine embroidery thread

20cm (8in) embroidery hoop

Thin black card

Equipment for mounting (see general instructions for card mounting, p138)

MAKING THE STAINED GLASS

Use a variety of different coloured fabrics, including plenty of blue shades. Include some silky fabrics to give a rich reflective effect.

Cut pieces into strips 6mm (¼in) wide and then across to make small rectangles.

Prepare your sewing machine for free machine embroidery (see general instructions for free machine embroidery, p140). Use a fine needle, a metallic thread on top and a neutral sewing thread below.

Stretch a piece of backing fabric in an embroidery hoop.

It is a good idea to place the different coloured fragments in groups round a board or plate and position this within easy reach of your sewing machine. Place some of these fragments onto the backing fabric and machine down using a spiralling motion (Fig 1). Continue to fix pieces of different colours, bringing in plenty of blue to make a good all-over effect.

Fig 1 Machining over the fragments using a spiralling motion

Begin by covering the backing fabric with random colours, then cut out the fretted card. To prepare the fret, trace the pattern. Add a little glue to the back of the tracing and position it accurately behind the central fold. Cut the fret through the tracing which can be gently peeled away afterwards. Place this over your work to give some idea of your progress. Continue to add fragments where necessary.

Finally, machine further into the work using smaller spirals to give the effect of stained glass.

Take the work out of the hoop and mount (see general information on card mounting, p138).

Alternative designs based on stained glass

SHADOW-QUILTED SNOWSCENE CARD

T his snowy little landscape is made from pieces of different coloured felt, positioned behind a transparent fabric. The design is back stitched through the layers, giving a quilted effect.

•

SIZE

15.4 x 17.8cm (6 x 7in)

•

MATERIALS

25cm (10in) square fine cotton backing fabric

25cm (10in) square white transparent fabric (cotton organdie)

Scraps of coloured felt:

dark blue (sky and cottage)

white (snow)

yellow (moon)

beige (path)

2 pale shades of stranded embroidery thread including yellow

20cm (8in) embroidery hoop

Fusible web (eg Bondaweb)

Tracing paper

Fabric transfer pencil

Coloured card

Equipment for mounting (see general instructions for card mounting, p138)

PREPARING THE FELT FOR SHADOW QUILTING

Each section of the pattern is a separate piece of felt (excluding smoke, windows, door and trees).

Start by tracing the design onto the backing fabric with a pencil or fabric transfer pencil.

Make another tracing, reversing the image. Use this and trace the separate sections of the design through onto the paper side of a piece of fusible web, leaving space round each. Cut out the fusible web patterns outside the line.

Iron each piece onto the correct coloured felt. Cut out the shapes very accurately along the line.

Peel away the paper on the fusible web and iron each piece onto the backing fabric, positioning each one carefully.

Cover the felt with the transparent fabric. Baste round the work just outside the rectangular edge of the design (the basting thread can then be left in place).

Place in an embroidery hoop.

Using a single strand of embroidery thread, back stitch (see Techniques and Stitches, p142) round each felt shape. The felt is sandwiched between the backing fabric and the transparent fabric, giving a slightly quilted effect.

Add the smoke to the chimney by couching 2 threads (see Techniques and Stitches, p142) and back stitch the details on the cottage.

Use thorn stitch (see Techniques and Stitches, p142) to embroider the fir trees with a yellow thread.

MAKING THE CARD

Take the work out of the hoop. Cut out the design leaving a 1cm (½in) border round the edge. Leave in the basting stitches.

Cut the card (see instructions for general mounting, p138), and position the snow scene.

Alternative design: after quilting add details such as eyes, beak, feathers, legs and footprints in surface stitchery

15.2in
(6in)

17.8cm (7in)

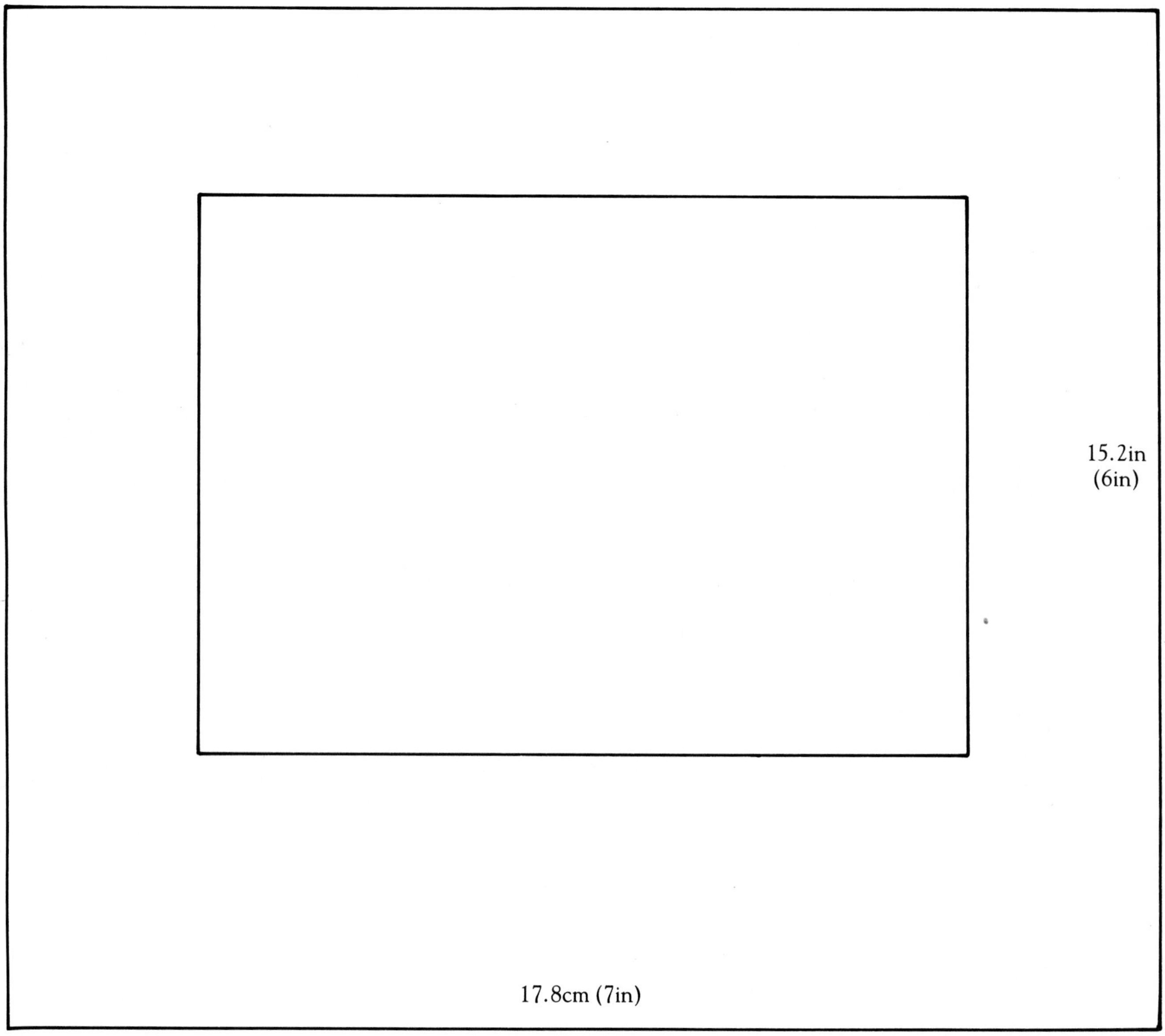

SHADOW-QUILTED SNOWFLAKE CARD

This smart card has a snowflake cut out of pelmet Vilene which is sandwiched between 2 layers of fabric, the top one being transparent. The snowflake is free machine stitched round the edge using a metallic thread.

•

SIZE

12.8cm (5in) square

•

MATERIALS

18cm (7in) square fine grey backing fabric

18cm (7in) square transparent fabric (shot organza is used for the snowflake in the photograph)

10cm (4in) square white non-woven pelmet stiffener (eg pelmet or craft quality Vilene)

10cm (4in) square fusible web (eg Bondaweb)

7 gold sequins

Gold metallic machine thread

12cm (5in) embroidery hoop

PVA adhesive

Coloured card

Equipment for mounting (see general instructions for card mounting, p138)

PREPARING THE SNOWFLAKE

Trace the snowflake pattern through onto the paper side of the square of Bondaweb.

Iron onto the pelmet stiffener (see manufacturer's instructions).

Cut out the snowflake very carefully with sharp pointed scissors.

Peel off the backing paper from the fusible web and iron the snowflake onto the grey backing fabric.

Position a sequin in the centre of the snowflake using a pinhead of adhesive. Glue a sequin onto the end of each bar.

Cover with the transparent fabric and baste the layers together round the snowflake.

Place the work in an embroidery hoop ready for free machine stitchery (see Techniques and Stitches, p140). Thread the machine with gold metallic thread and stitch round the edge of the snowflake.

MAKING THE CARD

Take the work out of the frame and trim to a 12cm (5in) square. Remove the basting stitches. Cut a square of card 9.5cm (3¾in). Place the work right side down on a flat surface and position the card centrally. Put a line of adhesive along one edge of the card and press a turning in place. Repeat with the other 3 turnings.

Cut the mounting card to the given size (see general instructions for card mounting, p138).

Glue the snowflake carefully onto the centre of the front fold to complete the card.

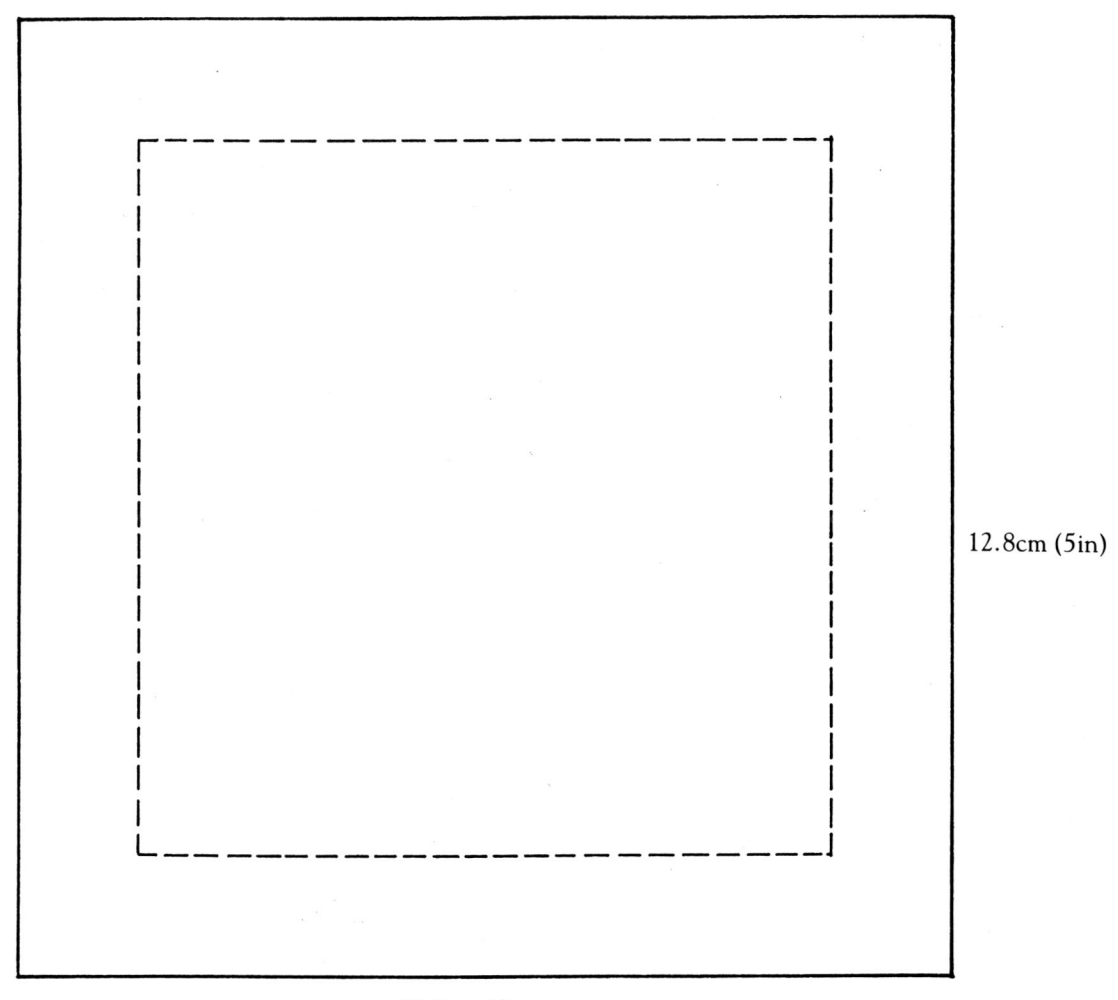

12.8cm (5in)

12.8cm (5in)

CANVASWORK STAR CARD

The star is worked on a fine canvas, and uses some metallic threads to make it rich and reflective.

•

SIZE

13.4 x 11.4cm (5¼ x 4½in)

•

MATERIALS

10cm (4in) square of canvas, 16 threads to 2.5cm (1in)

Skein of pale green coton perlé

Gold lurex crochet thread

Pink lurex crochet thread (or any other suitable metallic embroidery threads)

Fine tapestry needle

Small gold beads

Coloured card

Masking tape

Equipment for mounting (see general instructions for card mounting, p138)

WORKING THE EMBROIDERY

Bind the edges of the canvas with masking tape.

Find the centre of the canvas square and mark with a pin.

Begin the embroidery by working the central Rhodes stitch (Fig 1). Start by taking the needle from the front of the canvas to the back, leaving the knot on the surface beside the area to be covered with the Rhodes stitch. When enough stitches have been worked to secure the thread, the knot can be cut off.

To finish off a thread, run the needle through a few stitches at the back of the work and cut off.

Continue to follow the chart and work all the embroidery.

You may like to enrich your embroidery with some small beads sewn round the central Rhodes stitch.

Finally, cut away any surplus canvas to 1cm (½in) from the embroidery.

Mount behind the card (see general instructions for card mounting, p138).

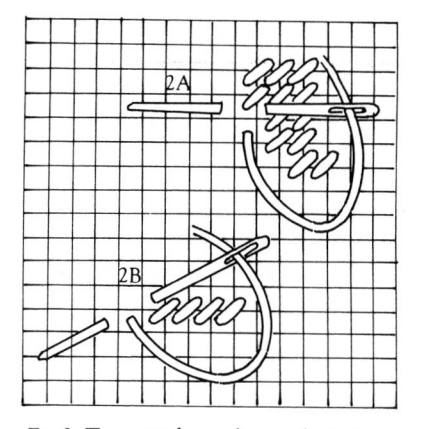

Fig 2 Tent stitch. a: diagonal stitches; b: horizontal stitches. Work the stitches diagonally whenever possible as this gives a better result

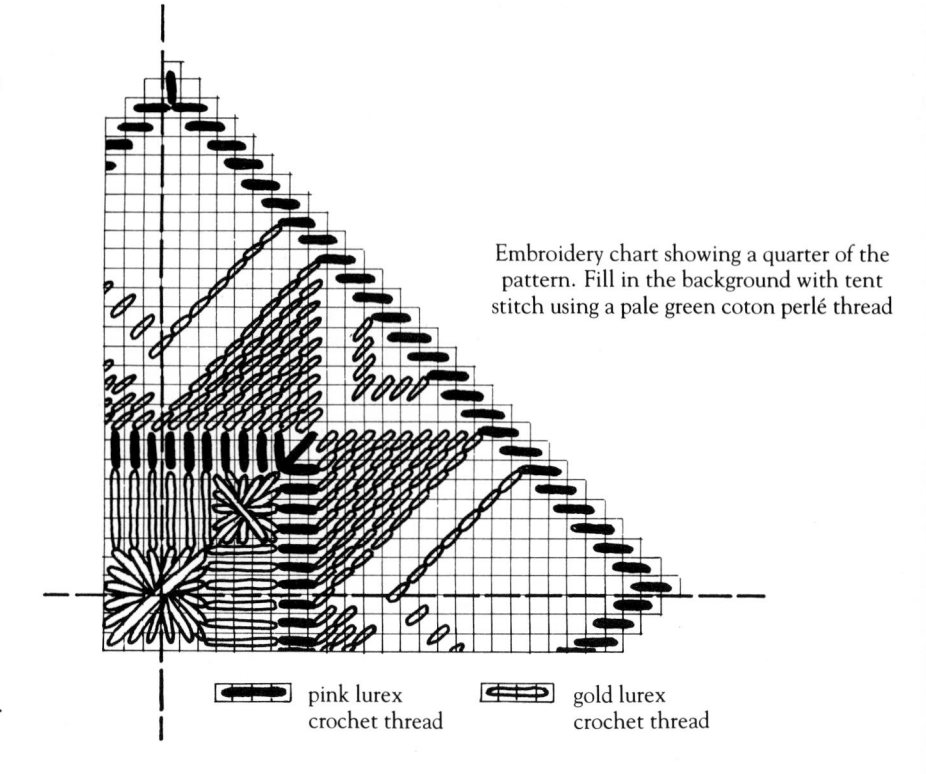

Embroidery chart showing a quarter of the pattern. Fill in the background with tent stitch using a pale green coton perlé thread

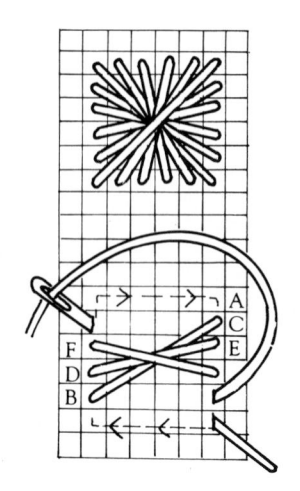

Fig 1 Rhodes stitch. Take the needle out at A, insert at B, out again at C and in at D. Continue round the four sides of the square

▭ pink lurex crochet thread   ▭ gold lurex crochet thread

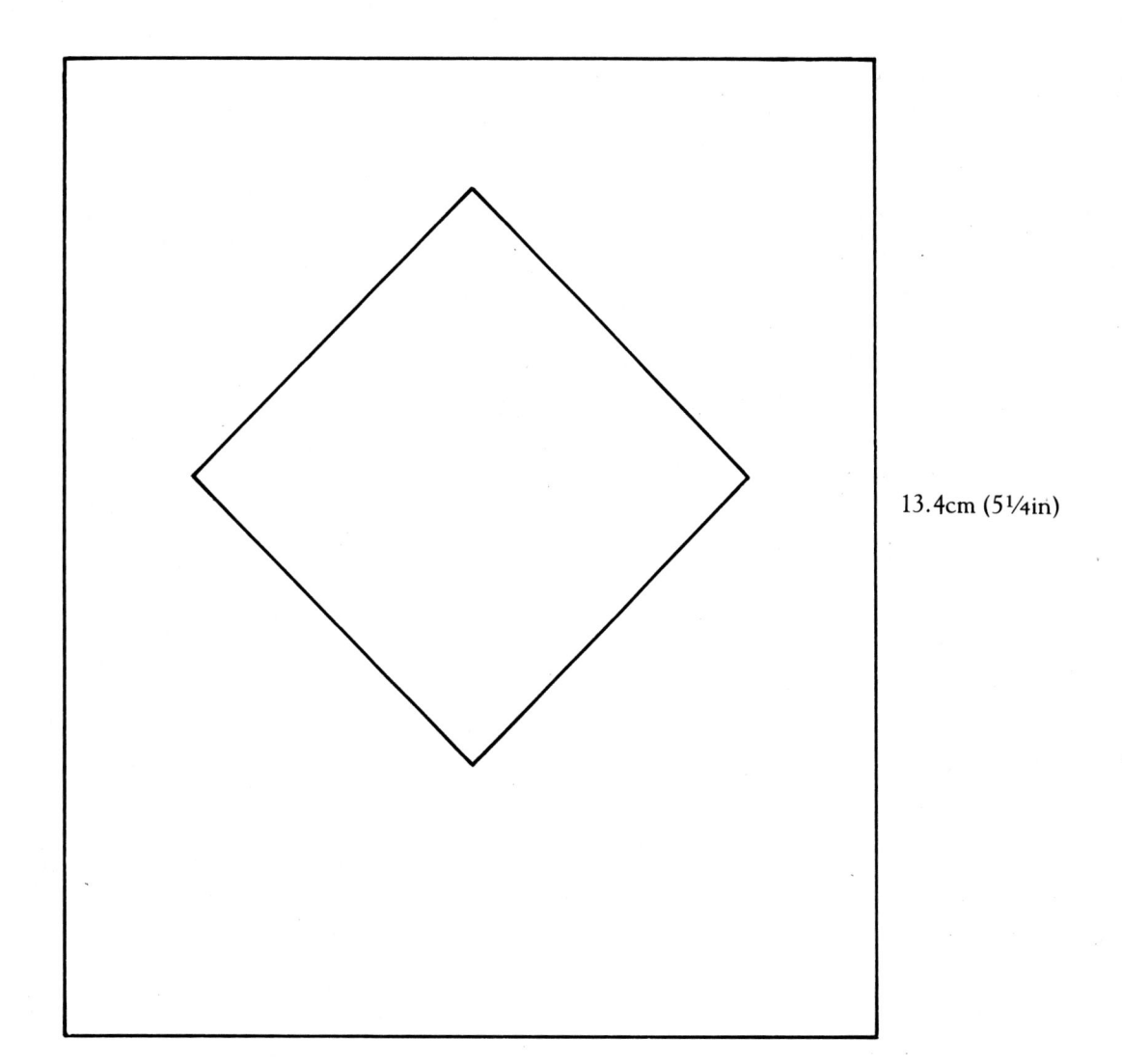

13.4cm (5¼in)

11.4cm (4½in)

FOLDED PATCHWORK TREE CARD

This simple little tree needs only a few stitches to complete. Pieces of fabric are folded and glued through the card.

•

SIZE

11.5 x 9cm (4½ x 3½in)

•

MATERIALS

Scraps of green fabric

Star-shaped sequin

PVA adhesive

Tracing paper and thin card for template

Thin white card

Equipment for mounting (see general instructions for card mounting, p138)

MAKING THE FOLDED PATCHWORK

Trace the pattern (Fig 1) and make a template (see Techniques and Stitches, p143).

Draw round the template on the green fabric 5 times. Cut out the rectangles along the marked line.

With each piece and with the wrong side facing, fold a 6mm (¼in) turning down along the top edge (a hot iron is useful during the folding process).

Bring point A to point C and point B to point C (Figs 1 and 2). Press the folds to make a triangle.

Cut out the card (see general instructions for card mounting, p138).

Mark all the slits in the central section (Fig 3) and cut them out using a craft knife.

Starting at the top of the tree, insert a triangle of fabric from the back of the card. Pull it through from the front, with the folded sides of the triangle facing, until it reaches the full extent of the slit. There will be a surplus of fabric below some of the slits which can be cut off to about 1cm (⅜in). Put a line of adhesive behind the trimmed fabric at the back of the card and press in place.

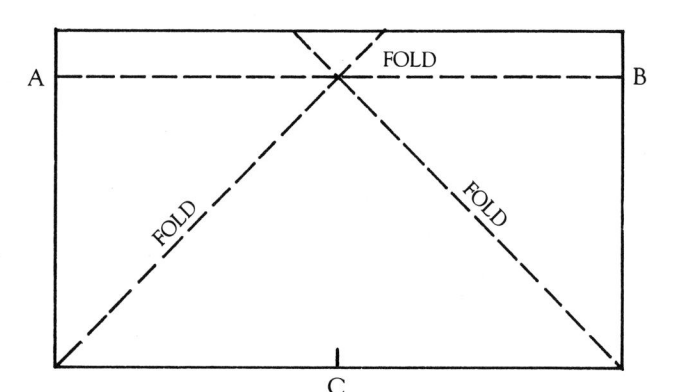

Fig 1 Pattern for folded triangle

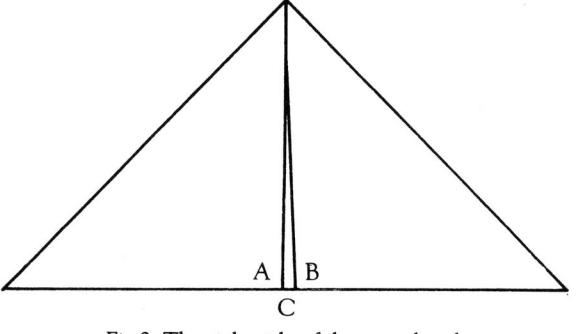

Fig 2 The right side of the completed triangle

95

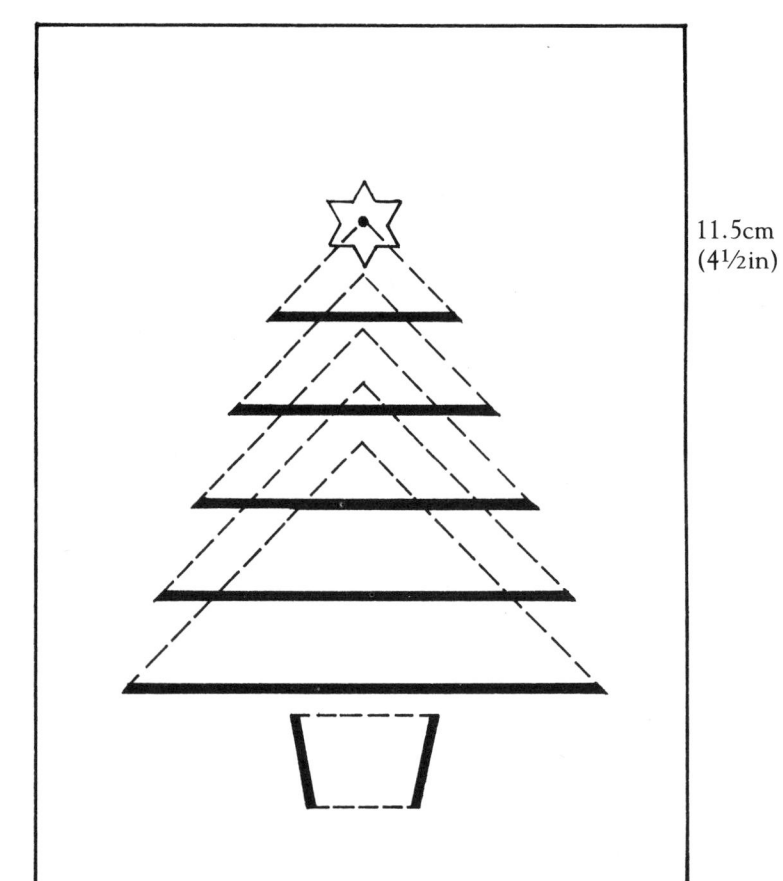

11.5cm
(4½in)

9cm (3½in)

Fig 3 Black areas represent slits and dotted
lines represent placement lines

Repeat with the other 4 triangles.
You can fix the points in place at
the front with a stitch through the
card.

Sew or glue a sequin at the top of
the tree.

MAKING THE BASE OF THE TREE

Trace and make a template of the base
of the tree (Fig 4). Cut out in fabric.

Fold the 4mm (⅛in) turnings at
the top and bottom to the back. Press.

Insert through the slits and glue in
place at the back of the card.

Complete the card (see general
instructions for card mounting, p138).

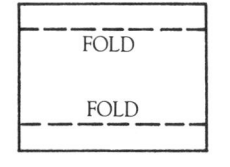

Fig 4 Tree base

FOLDED PATCHWORK STAR CARD

This card uses a popular patchwork technique to create a dramatic Christmas star. Very little stitchery is involved, but accuracy is essential in the folding and positioning of the fabric triangles.

•

SIZE

15.2 x 12.7cm (6 x 5in)

MATERIALS

Small quantities of 3 contrasting fine cotton seasonal fabrics (silks would also be suitable)

A square of fine cotton foundation fabric

Coloured card

Equipment for mounting (see general instructions for card mounting, p138)

Thin card and tracing paper for template

MAKING THE FOLDED PATCHWORK

Rectangles are cut and folded to make triangles. Trace the pattern (Fig 1) and make a template (see Techniques and Stitches, p143).

Take one of the fabrics and draw round the template 4 times. Cut out the rectangles along the marked line.

With each piece and with the wrong side facing, fold a 6mm (¼in) turning down along the top edge (a hot iron is useful during the folding process).

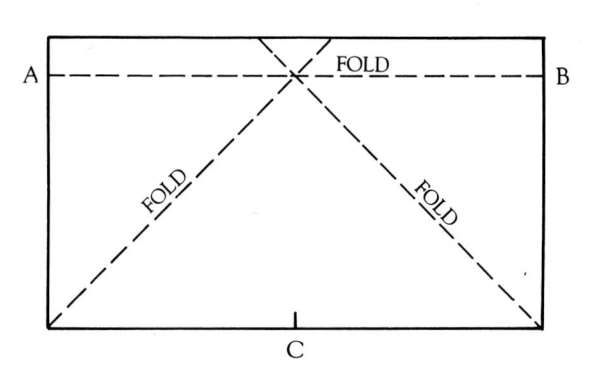

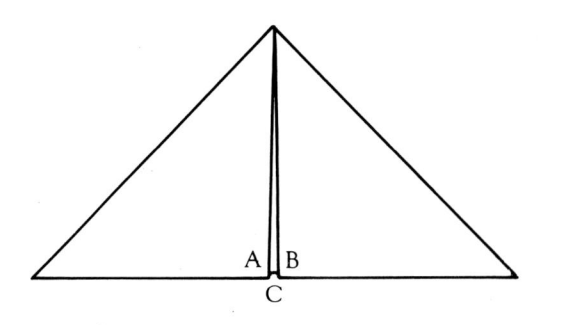

Fig 1 Pattern for folded triangle

Fig 2 The right side of the completed triangle

Bring point A to point C and point B to C (Figs 1 and 2). Press the folds to make a triangle. Repeat with the other 2 fabrics, making 8 triangles from each.

Now prepare the foundation fabric. Use the placement illustration (p100) as a guide and draw the square on the fabric. Mark the horizontal, vertical and diagonal lines – these are placement lines for the triangles.

Take the first 4 triangles and position them onto the foundation fabric so that the points meet at the centre (Figs 3 and 4).

Use a suitable sewing thread and make an invisible stitch at each point to catch the triangles down to the foundation fabric. Work running stitches close to the lower edge of the triangles.

Take 4 triangles of the second colour and position them over the first 4 (Fig 5).

It is a good idea at this stage to trace the placement guide (p100) and to place the tracing over the work from time to time to ensure the correct positioning of the triangles. Great accuracy is needed if the patchwork is to look good behind the card mount.

Stitch the triangles down onto the foundation fabric in the same manner. Place and stitch the final 4 of the second colour along the diagonal lines (Fig 6).

Repeat the process with the 8 triangles in the third colour using the placement tracing.

Cut the card (see instructions for general card mounting, p138), and position the patchwork.

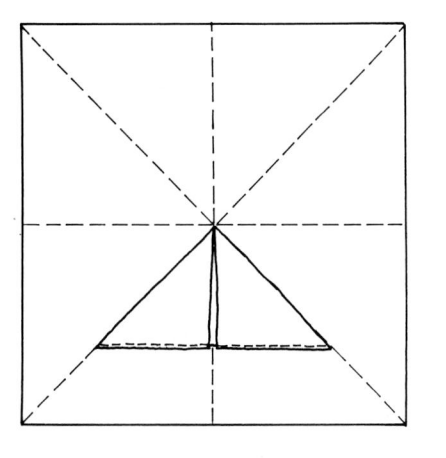

Fig 3 One triangle

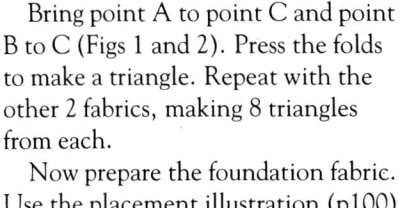

Fig 4 Four triangles

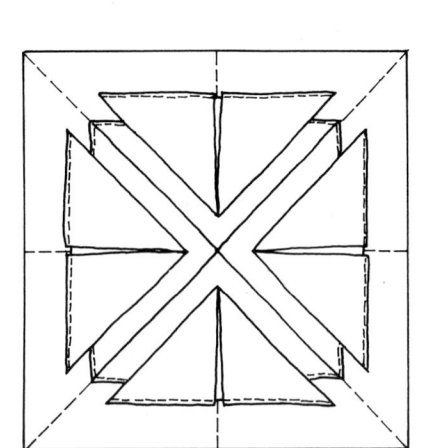

Fig 5 Eight triangles

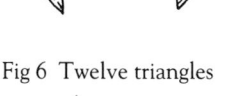

Fig 6 Twelve triangles

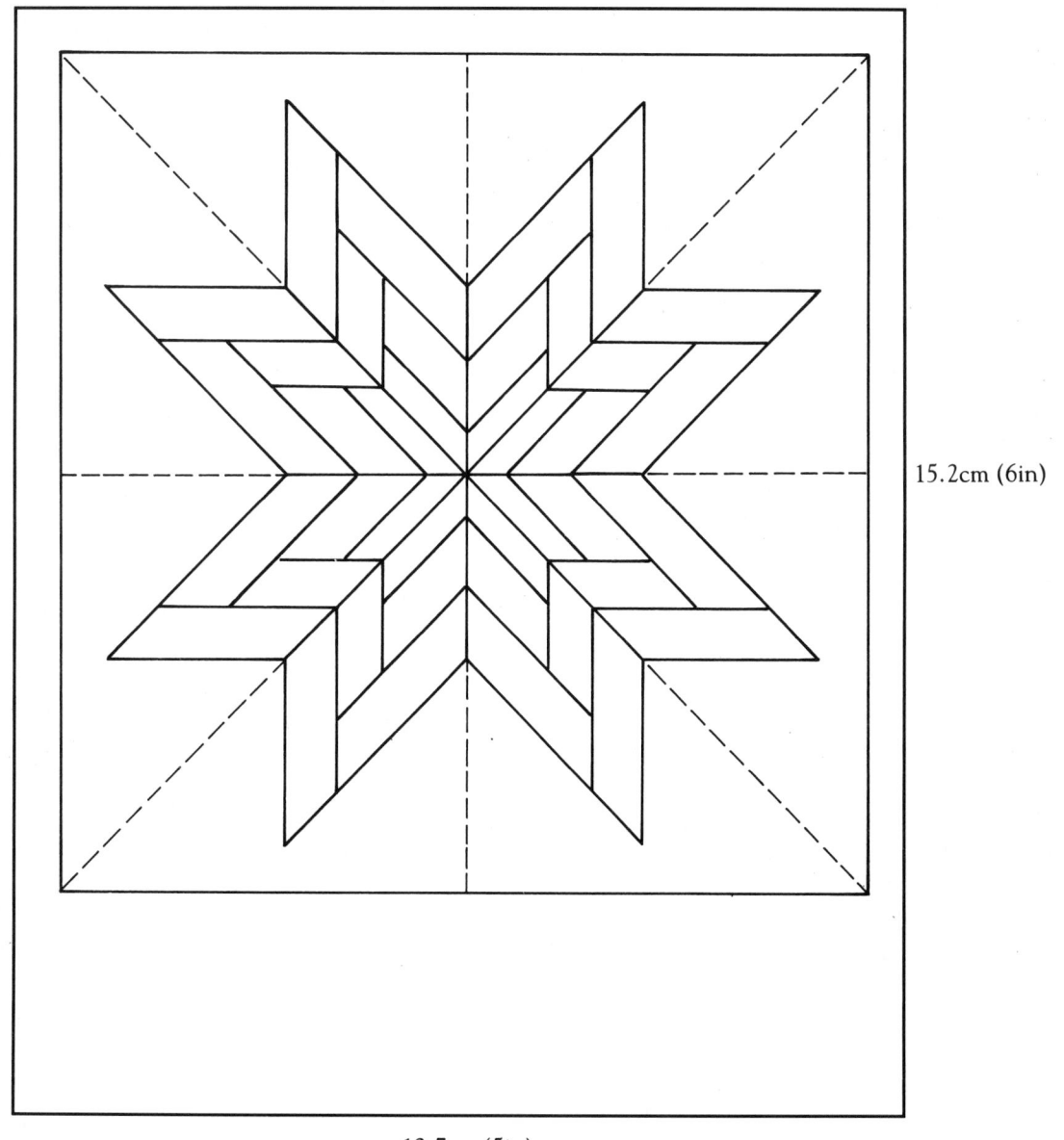

15.2cm (6in)

12.7cm (5in)

Showing placement lines for folded triangles

MACHINE-EMBROIDERED CARDS

These three cards can be made very quickly, which is an obvious advantage during the busy time of Christmas. The machine embroidery can be done in strips, cut up to the required size and mounted behind card.

SIZE
15.5 x 11.5cm (6 x 4½in)

MATERIALS

10cm (4in) long strips of red and green felt

Gold metallic machine thread

Small gold beads

Coloured card

Equipment for mounting (see general instructions for card mounting, p138)

PREPARING THE STITCHERY

Thread the machine up with metallic thread. The stitchery consists of rows of straight and zigzag stitches of different widths and lengths. If your machine can do other decorative stitches, then try these. In any case, it is advisable to experiment on a piece of fabric before you attempt to work the finished strips. Use the sewing foot as a gauge between rows.

When you have chosen a successful arrangement of stitches, work the strips.

MAKING THE CARDS

Cut the cards to the given size (see general instructions for card mounting, p138).

Cut the strips of felt into rectangles to fit behind the chosen mounts – for example, tree, bauble or stocking.

The obvious advantage is that several cards can be made at the same time. Add a hanging ribbon to the bauble card. Decorate some rows of zigzag with small gold beads.

Complete the cards (see general mounting instructions, p138).

PATTERN

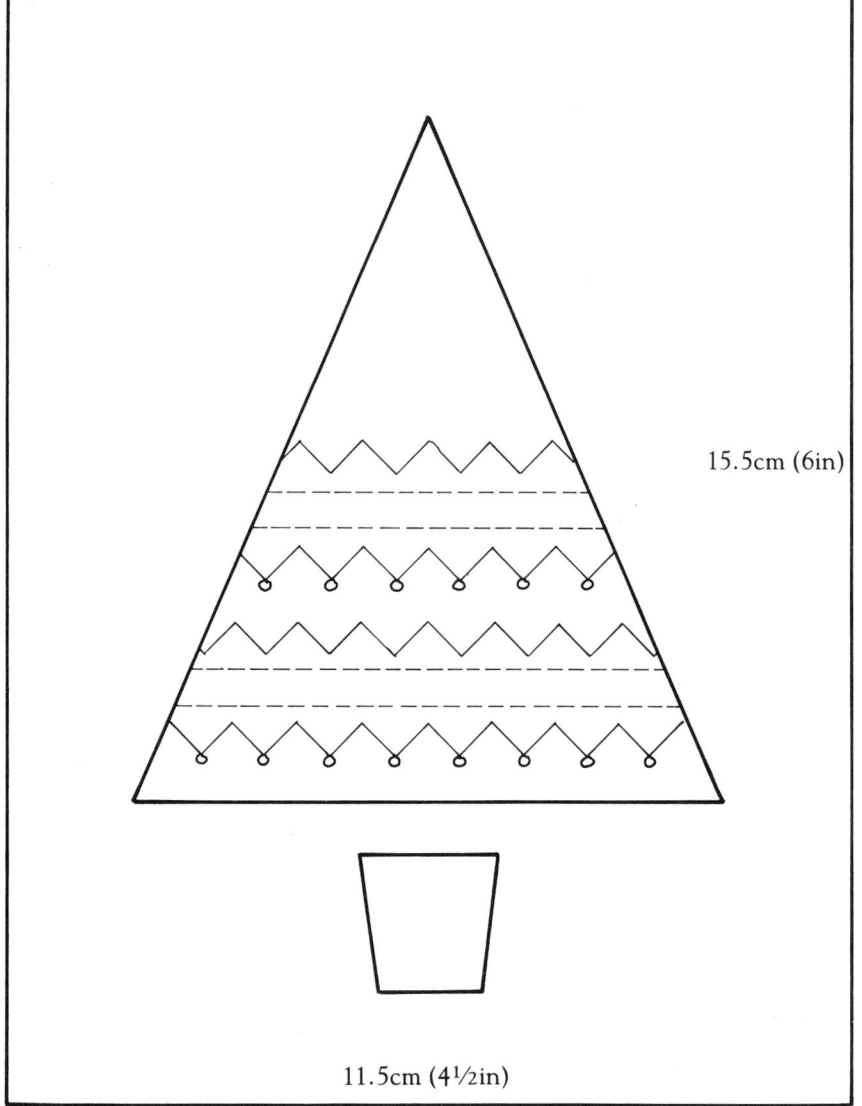

15.5cm (6in)

11.5cm (4½in)

101

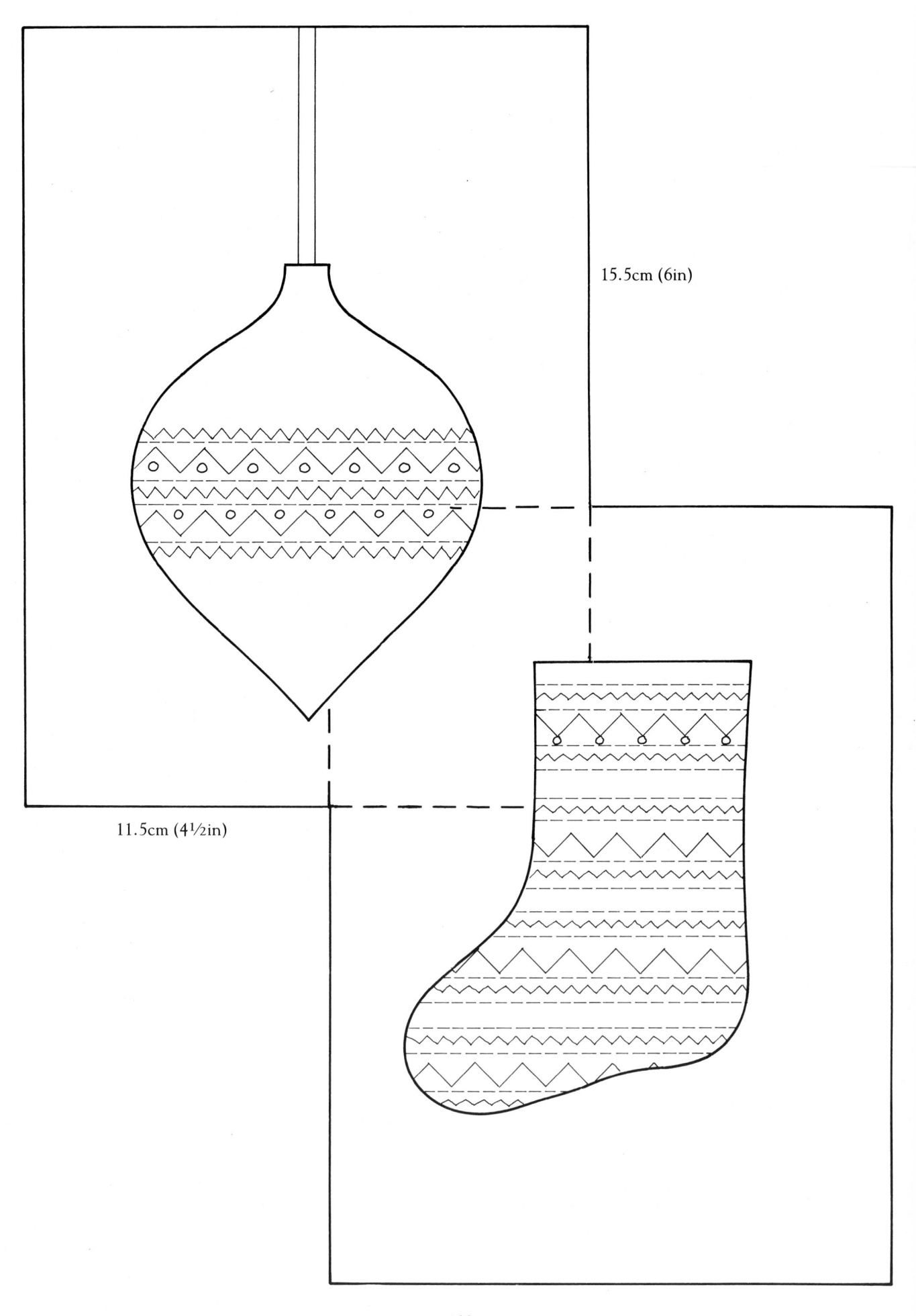

15.5cm (6in)

11.5cm (4½in)

WRAPPED TREE CARD

The secret of this little tree is double-sided adhesive tape which holds the wrapped and beaded threads in place.

•

SIZE

12 x 10.5cm (4¾ x 4¼in)

•

MATERIALS

Thin white card

Skein of white coton perlé

Double-sided adhesive tape

Fine silver thread (metallic machine thread)

Small silver beads

Coloured card

Equipment for mounting (see general instructions for card mounting, p138)

MAKING THE TREE

Trace the tree pattern and cut out in thin white card (see Techniques and Stitches, p138).

Cut short strips of adhesive tape. On the front and back of the card stick strips around the edges and down the centre including the trunk (Fig 1). Trim off the overlaps.

Peel away the backing paper from the tape.

Start the wrapping at the top of the tree. Take the end of the white thread and press it down onto the tape at the back 2cm (1in) below the top point (Fig 1).

Then, starting at the point, wrap the thread carefully round the card, pressing the threads onto the tape as you go. Make sure that the threads do not overlap.

Continue down and wrap the trunk. Finish by securing the end with a small piece of adhesive tape.

PATTERN

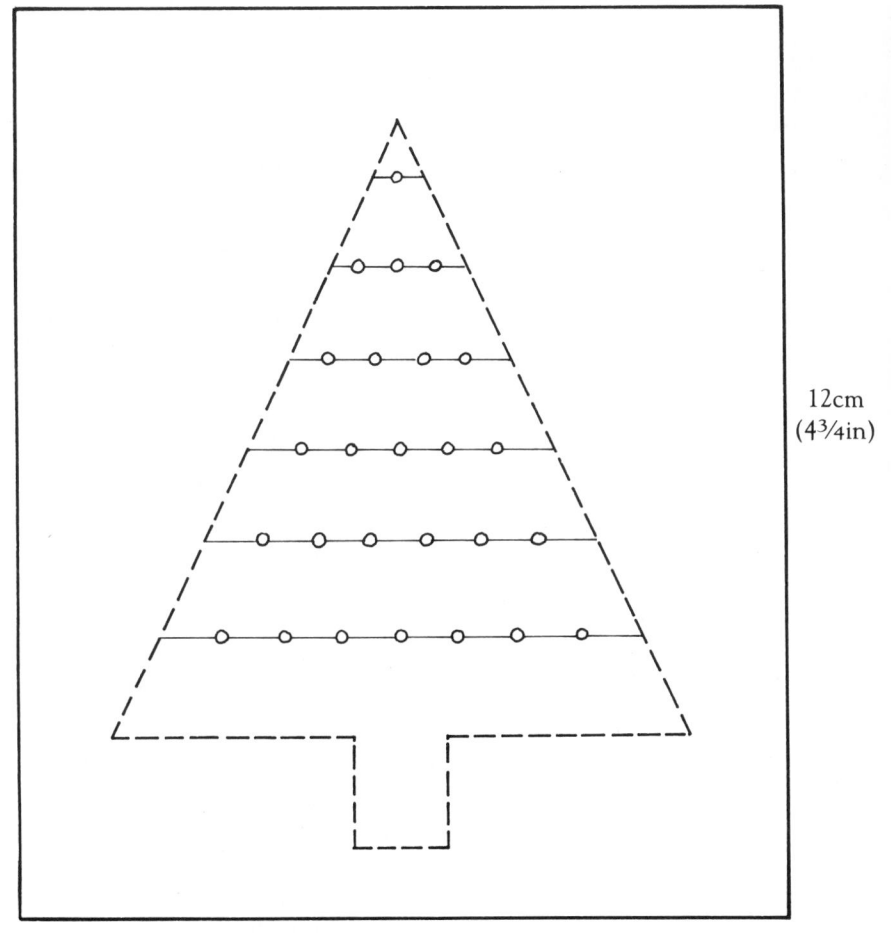

12cm (4¾in)

10.5cm (4¼in)

Fig 1 Showing the positioning of the adhesive tape and the start of the wrapping on the back of the tree.

The tree has 6 rows of threaded beads.

Take the end of the silver thread and attach with adhesive tape to the back of the tree just below the top. Bring the thread to the front. Thread on a bead (see Hearts and Stars, p38) and take the thread across and round to the back.

Bring the thread to the front 12mm (½in) down the tree. Thread on 3 beads and take the thread across and round to the back.

Repeat 4 times more with 4 beads,

5 beads, 6 beads and 7 beads respectively. Secure the thread with tape at the back of the tree and cut off.

Cut the mounting card to the correct size (see general instructions for card mounting, p138).

The completed tree can then either be glued in position or more double-sided adhesive tape can be cut to size and fixed to the back. Peel away the backing paper and press it down onto the front fold of the card in its correct position.

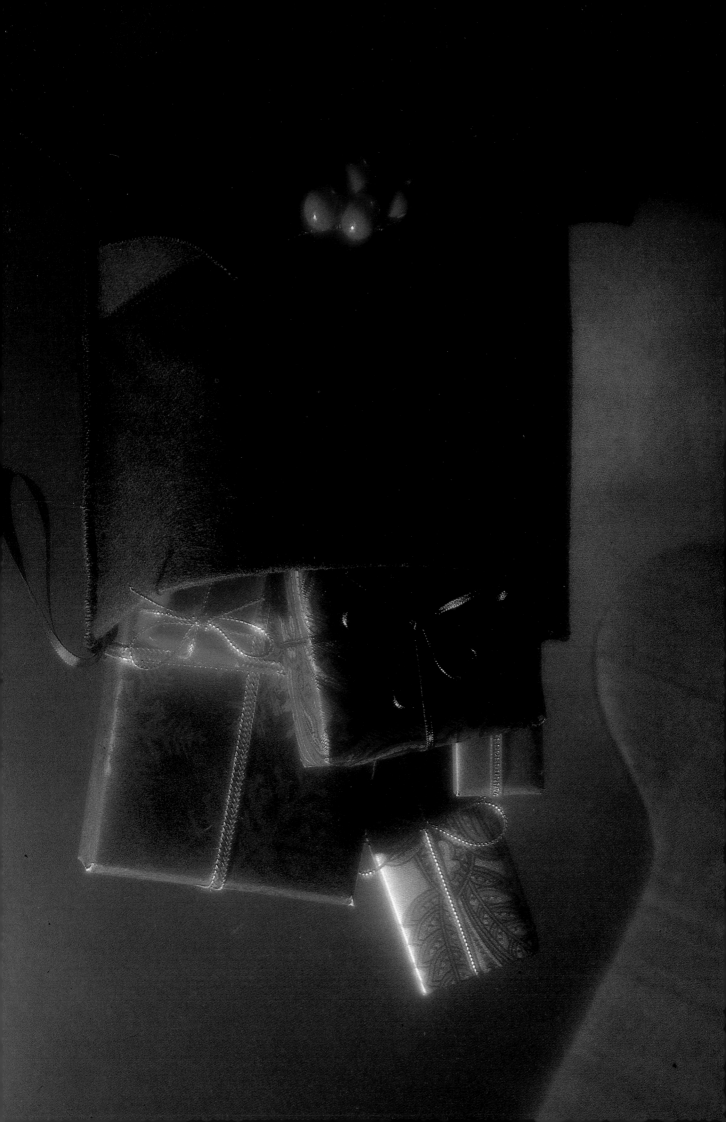

Stockings

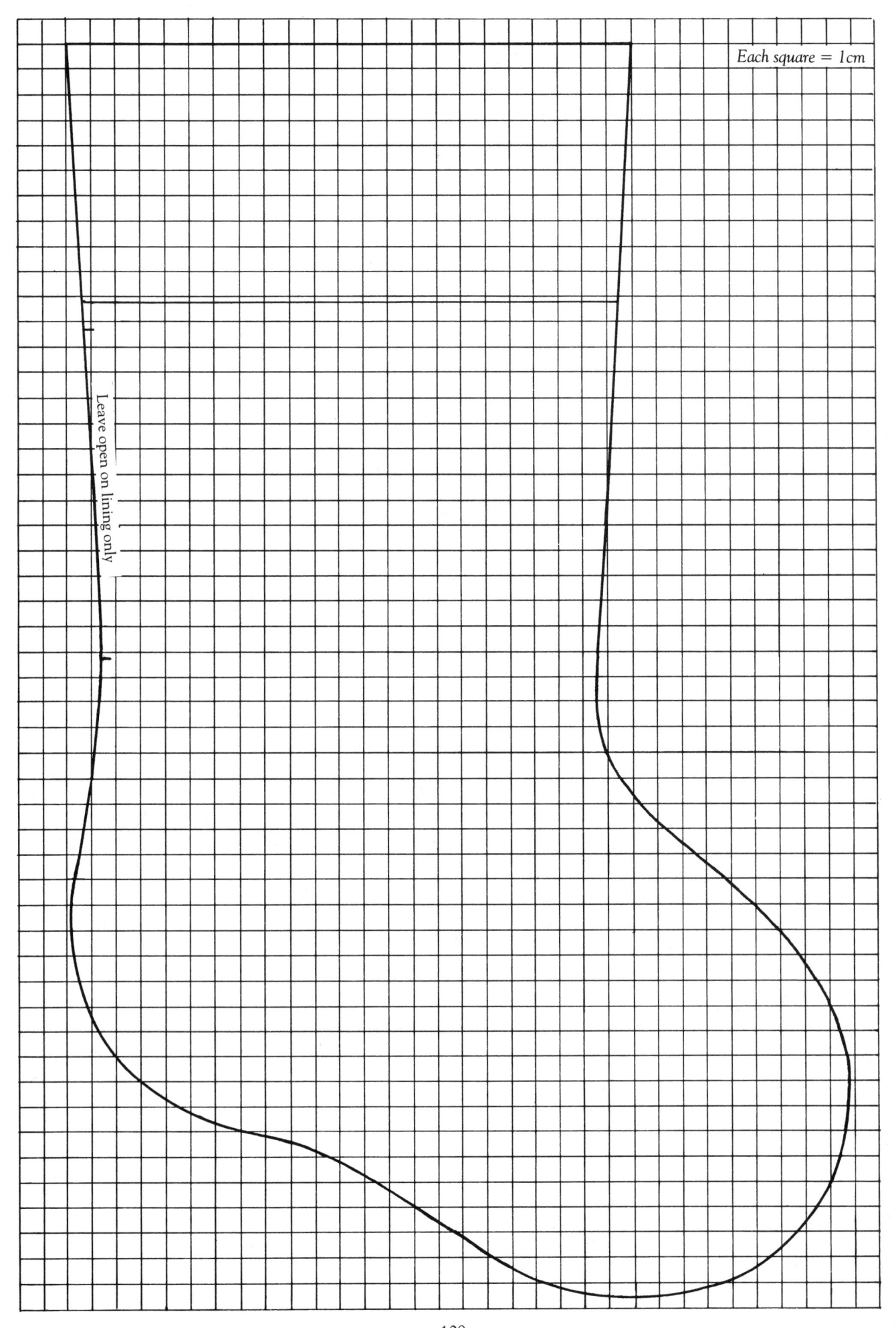

Each square = 1cm

Leave open on lining only

FELT STOCKING

This attractive stocking is very quick and easy to make.

APPROXIMATE SIZE

50cm (19½in)

MATERIALS

64 x 69cm (25 x 27in) dark green felt

Matching machine thread

54 x 69cm (21 x 27in) light green felt

Fusible web (eg Bondaweb)

4 red wooden beads approximately 1.2cm (½in) in diameter

20cm (8in) of approximately 1.5cm (⅝in) wide dark green ribbon

Graph paper (1cm) and thin card for template

The stocking is made from 2 layers of felt. The dark green lining extends to include the cuff which is folded over onto the right side of the stocking. The layers of felt are fused together with fusible web. The stocking could be made with just 1 layer of felt with the cuff stitched on top. This would make a less expensive but also a less substantial stocking.

Enlarge the stocking pattern on p108 and make a template (see Techniques and Stitches, pp140 and 143). Draw a line on the template for the cuff, 10cm (4in) down from the top edge of the stocking. Make sure that the line is parallel to the top edge.

Make the stocking front the exact size of the template. Add about 12mm (½in) down the sides and round the foot of the stocking back. Do not add extra to the top edge. This extra 12mm (½in) will be cut away at a later stage.

Draw round the template twice onto the smooth (paper) side of the fusible web reversing the template to make a pair. Add the extra 12mm (½in) round the stocking back. Iron onto the light green felt and cut out.

Draw a pair of cuffs on the fusible web adding an extra 12mm (½in) to the sides of the back cuff only. Place the fusible web cuffs on the dark green felt with the bottom edges of the cuffs against one 69cm (27in) edge of the felt. Remove the paper backing from the front and back stockings and place them on the dark green felt. Match the top edges of stockings to the top edges of the cuffs (Fig 1). Iron the cuffs in place. Use a dry iron and damp cloth to fuse the stockings to the dark green felt.

Cut out each stocking and cuff all in one piece. Do not cut along the top edge of the stockings. Remove the paper backing from the cuffs and fold them over onto the light green felt. Fuse the cuffs to the top of the stockings. Zigzag over the bottom edge of the cuffs using dark green machine thread.

Pin the front and back stockings together, right sides out, carefully matching the top edges. Zigzag all round over the edge of the stocking front leaving the top edge open. Trim

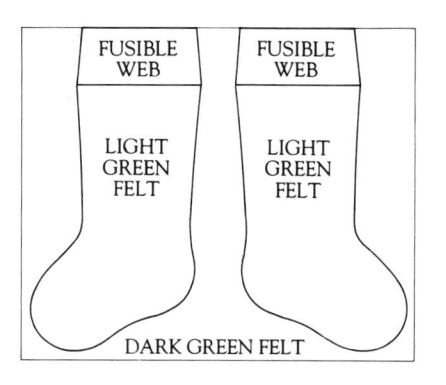

Fig 1 Cutting layout for felt stocking

the stocking back close to the stitching. Zigzag round the stocking, again using a slightly wider stitch.

Cut a piece of ribbon 20cm (8in) long to make a hanging loop. Fold it in half and turn the ends under to neaten. Stitch the loop securely to the inside top of the back seam.

Trace the holly leaf pattern and make a template. Make 3 holly leaves following the instructions for the Tree Skirt (see p42). Sew the leaves together to form a spray and add 4 red wooden beads for the berries. Stitch the spray to the front of the stocking at the centre of the bottom edge of the cuff.

PATTERN FOR HOLLY LEAF

A - B

RANDOM PATCHWORK STOCKING

This rich gorgeous stocking is made from scraps of a variety of red fabrics.

•

APPROXIMATE SIZE

50cm (19½in)

•

MATERIALS

Scraps of red dress-weight fabrics

56 x 76cm (22 x 30in) backing fabric (old sheets will do)

56 x 76cm (22 x 30in) red lining fabric

Red machine thread

20cm (8in) of approximately 1.5cm (⅝in) wide red ribbon

Graph paper (1cm) and thin card for template

GENERAL INSTRUCTIONS

The fabric scraps are stitched to a backing so it is possible to mix silk, satin, cotton and lining fabrics. Use fabrics of a similar weight. Thick heavy fabrics are not suitable. For a rich effect include silks and satins. Press all the fabrics before you begin.

Triangular scraps were used to make the red stocking. You might find it easier to use a mixture of triangular and irregular four-sided shapes. The edges of the scraps must be straight; it is impossible to use curved shapes for this technique. Vary the size and shape of the scraps to make an attractive design. Do not use the same fabrics side by side.

The method of working random patchwork is similar to strip patchwork. All the scraps, except the first, are machined on the wrong side

and then folded and pressed to the right side. The scraps are stitched so that they overlap each other. No raw edges should be visible. Machine only one edge of a scrap before pressing to the right side. If two sides are stitched, it is impossible to fold the scrap over. When machining the seams leave a 6mm (¼in) seam allowance. Use the machine presser foot as a guide.

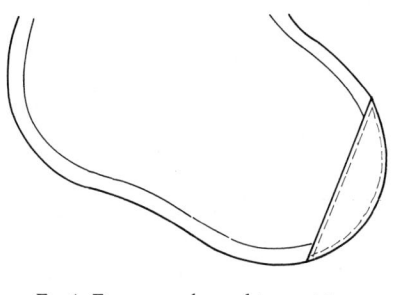

Fig 1 First scrap basted in position

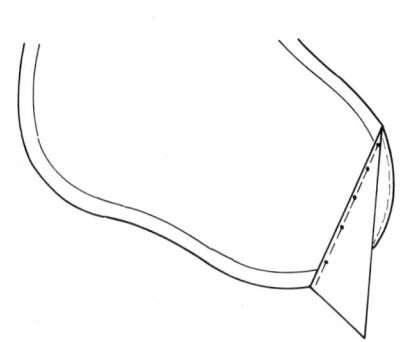

Fig 2 Second scrap pinned in position

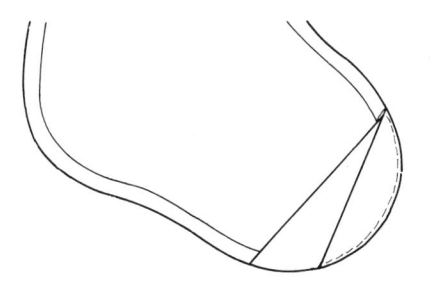

Fig 3 Second scrap pressed to the right side

MAKING THE STOCKING

Enlarge the stocking pattern on p108 and make a template (see Techniques and Stitches, pp140 and 143). Press all the fabrics before you begin.

Draw round the template twice on the backing fabric, reversing the template to make a pair. This is the stitching line. Add a 2.5cm (1in) seam allowance all round. Cut out both pieces. It is helpful to see the

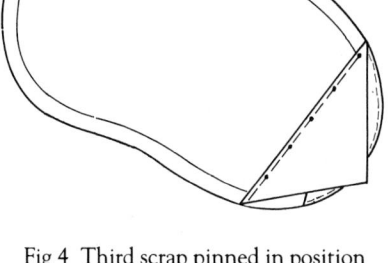

Fig 4 Third scrap pinned in position

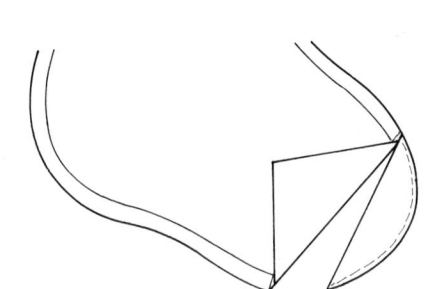

Fig 5 Third scrap pressed to the right side

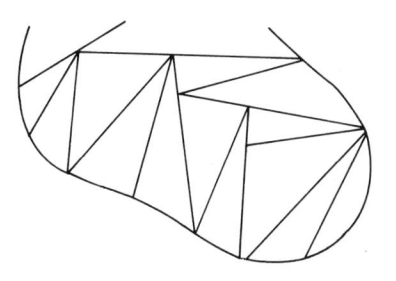

Fig 6 Foot of stocking completed

stitching line on both sides of the fabric, so machine or baste all round on the stitching line of each backing piece. Draw a line on the backing, parallel to the top edge of each stocking. Draw the line 9.5cm (3¾in) down from the top edge.

Begin the patchwork at the toe of the stocking. Smooth the fabrics as you work.

Place the first scrap on the backing fabric, right side up, making sure that it extends into the seam allowance. Pin and baste to the backing (Fig 1).

Place the second scrap, right side down, on top of the first with the edges matching. Pin through all the layers on the stitching line (Fig 2). Fold to the right side to check that it is the shape you want before

machining 6mm (¼in) from the edge. Press to the right side (Fig 3). Add the third scrap in the same way (Figs 4 and 5). Continue adding scraps (Fig 6), making sure that the patchwork extends into the seam allowance.

End the random patchwork on the drawn line 9.5cm (3¾in) from the top edge. Cut a strip of fabric 12cm (4¾in) wide and 26cm (10¼in) long for the cuff. Place the cuff right side down on the patchwork with the edge on the drawn line. Pin and machine through all the layers on the stitching line. Press to the right side and baste the top and side edges to the backing.

Make the stocking back in the same way. (If you are short of time, use a piece of plain fabric for the back.)

LINING THE STOCKING

Working from the back, zigzag all round the stocking, just inside the seam allowance.

Draw round the template twice on the wrong side of the lining fabric, reversing the template to make a pair. Add a 12mm (½in) seam allowance all round. Cut out the stocking lining.

Line the stocking following the instructions for the hessian stocking (see p113). Clip the curves on the patchwork stocking and on the lining before turning to the right side.

Cut a piece of ribbon 20cm (8in) long to make a hanging loop. Fold in half and turn the ends under to neaten. Stitch the loop securely to the inside top of the back seam.

HESSIAN STOCKING

The hessian is richly decorated with couched ribbons, braids and threads which form a 'cuff' all round the top of the stocking.

•

APPROXIMATE SIZE

50cm (19½in)

•

MATERIALS

56 x 76cm (22 x 30in) cream hessian

56 x 76cm (22 x 30in) cream lining fabric

Cream machine thread

Selection of the following in red, green and gold:

Embroidery threads, narrow ribbons, narrow braids and thick yarns

Red and gold beads

Graph paper (1cm) and thin card for template

Enlarge the pattern on p108 and make a template (see Techniques and Stitches, pp140 and 143).

The top edge of the stocking must be straight along the grain of the hessian. Draw round the template twice on the back of the hessian, reversing the template to make a pair. This is the stitching line. Add a 2.5cm (1in) seam allowance all round. To prevent the hessian from fraying, zigzag round the seam allowance before cutting out. Baste along the stitching line at the top of the stocking.

COUCHING

The decorative 'cuff' at the top of the stocking consists of rows of couched threads, ribbons and braids. The threads etc are laid on the surface of the fabric and held in place with stitches using another thread, the couching thread.

A number of stitches are suitable for couching, including blanket stitch (Fig 1) and herringbone stitch (Fig 2). The stitches can be varied by altering

the spaces between them (Figs 1 and 2). The couching stitches are worked into the hessian on each side of the ribbon etc.

Use a variety of gold, green and red ribbons, braids and threads to create a very rich effect. Mix different widths and textures and include plenty of gold thread. The 'couched' ribbons etc need be only 28cm (11in) long, so it is a good opportunity to use up oddments from the ragbag.

Hessian is loosely woven and it is possible to count the threads, which helps to space the stitches evenly. Use a tapestry needle for the stitching and work the stitches in the gaps between the threads. Keep the rows straight by following the threads in the hessian.

Begin the couching just below the basted line at the top of the stocking. Cut a piece of ribbon, braid or thick yarn and hold it in place with a row of blanket or herringbone stitch. Begin and end the rows of stitching with a couple of back stitches well into the seam allowance. Do not pull the couching thread too tight as you stitch.

Continue couching ribbons etc until the decorative 'cuff' is 10cm (4in) deep. Work a similar 'cuff' on the back of the stocking.

Sew 2 or 3 rows of small gold or red beads between the couched ribbons etc on each side of the stocking. Do not sew beads too close to the side edges at this stage because they will get in the way of the machine when the stocking is made up. They can be added later. Zigzag all round each of the hessian stocking pieces just inside the seam allowance.

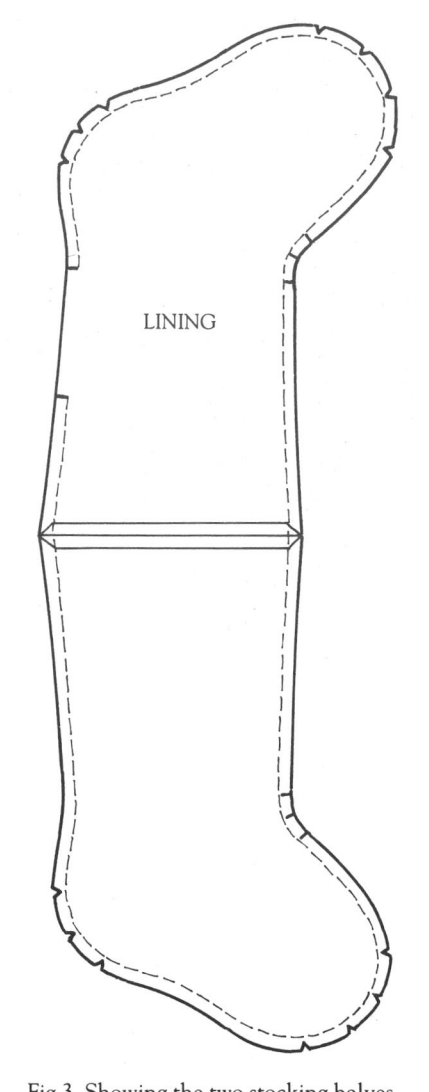

LINING

LINING THE STOCKING

Draw round the template twice on the back of the lining fabric, reversing the template to make a pair. Add a 12mm (½in) seam allowance all round.

Place 1 hessian stocking piece and 1 lining piece right sides together. Make sure that the stitching lines match. Pin and machine across the top of the stocking using cream thread. Trim the seam allowance on the hessian to 12mm (½in) and press the seam open. Repeat with the other stocking pieces.

Pin the 2 stocking halves together, right sides facing, carefully matching the stitching lines (Fig 3). Machine all round, leaving an opening in the lining as shown on the pattern. Trim the seam allowance to about 1cm (⅜in), but do not cut through the zigzag stitches on the hessian. Clip the curves on the lining only. It should not be necessary on the hessian.

Turn to the right side and slip stitch the opening. Press the stocking and push the lining inside. Press the top edge carefully.

Make a twisted cord 140cm (55in) long (see Techniques and Stitches p143). Use a mixture of gold, red and green threads and make the cord about 4mm (³⁄₁₆in) thick. Pin the neat (folded) end of the cord to the top of

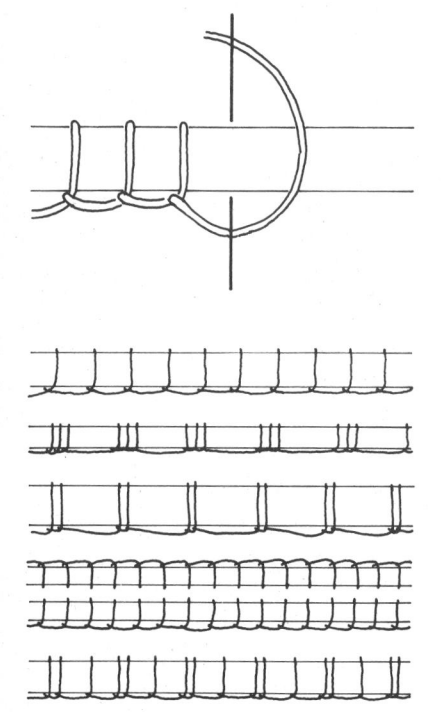

Fig 1 Blanket stitch used for couching ribbons etc

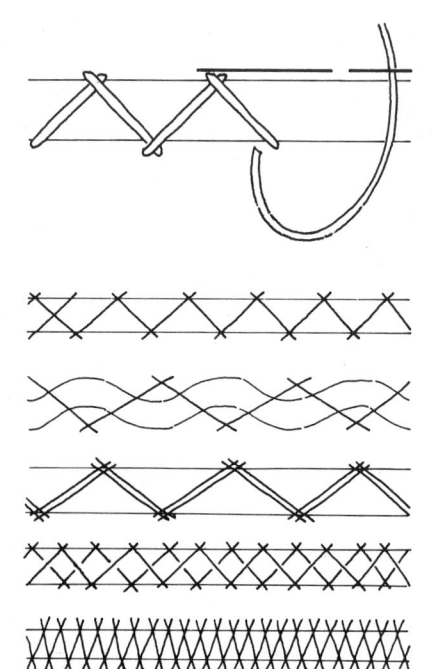

Fig 2 Herringbone stitch used for couching ribbons etc

Fig 3 Showing the two stocking halves stitched together

the front seam. Slip stitch the cord all round the stocking to the top of the back seam. Make a hanging loop with the last few centimetres (inches) of the cord, tucking the knotted end into the stocking. For a really neat finish, unpick the lining seam near the hanging loop and tuck the end in there. Slip stitch the gap. Make sure that the hanging loop is really secure by stitching through the cord to the top of the stocking several times. Fasten off securely.

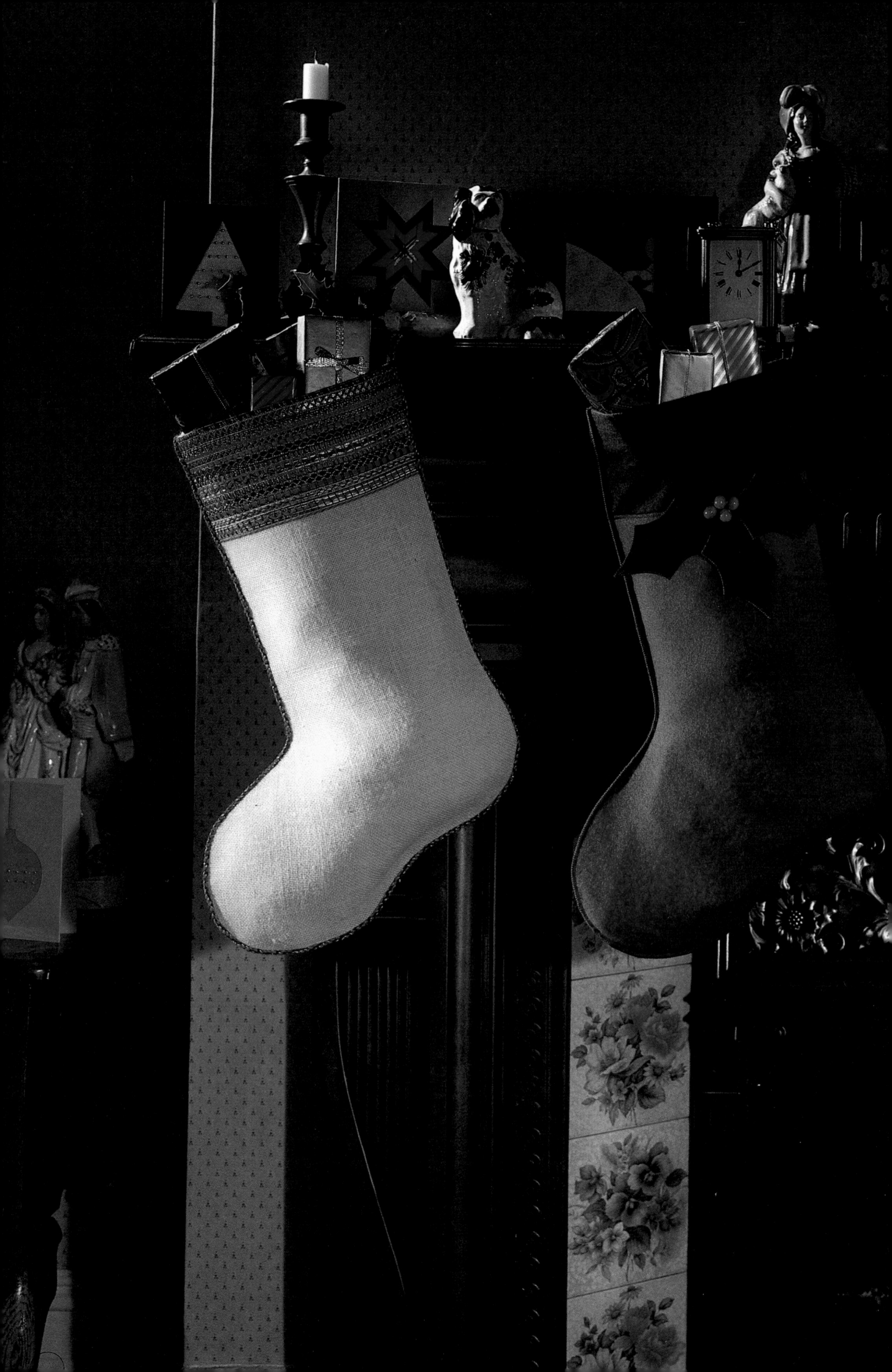

STRIP PATCHWORK STOCKING

Cream strip patchwork, decorated with lace and machine stitching, makes a very attractive stocking for a teenage girl.

•

APPROXIMATE SIZE

50cm (19½in)

•

MATERIALS

Selection of cream dress-weight fabrics

56 x 76cm (22 x 30in) backing fabric (old sheets will do)

56 x 76cm (22 x 30in) cream lining fabric

Cream machine thread

Fine metallic gold machine thread

Cream lace approximately 12mm (½in) wide

20cm (8in) of approximately 1.5cm (⅝in) wide cream ribbon

Graph paper (1cm) and thin card for template

Enlarge the stocking pattern on p108 and make a template (see Techniques and Stitches, pp140 and 143).

PREPARING THE PATCHWORK STRIPS

Choose a variety of cream fabrics of similar weight. Thick heavy fabrics are not suitable – use dress-weight cottons and silks etc. Press all the fabrics before you begin. Cut the fabric along the grain. Accurate cutting and stitching are essential for a good finish.

One strip 12cm (4¾in) wide and 25cm (10in) long is needed for the cuff on each side of the stocking. Use the same fabric for the back and front cuffs if possible.

Cut the other strips 2.5-4cm (1-1½in) wide. This includes a 6mm (¼in) seam allowance on each side of the strip. The finished width of the strips will be about 1.2-2.5cm (½-1in).

The lengths needed vary from approximately 24cm (9½in) at the narrowest part of the stocking to approximately 34cm (13½in) at the widest part. Cut the lengths as you need them to avoid waste.

PREPARING THE BACKING FABRIC

The strips of cream fabric are stitched to a backing fabric.

Draw round the template twice on the backing fabric, reversing the template to make a pair. This is the stitching line. Add about a 2.5cm (1in) seam allowance all round. Cut out both pieces. It is helpful to see the stitching line on both sides of the backing fabric, so machine or baste all round on the stitching line of each backing piece.

Draw feint pencil lines at intervals

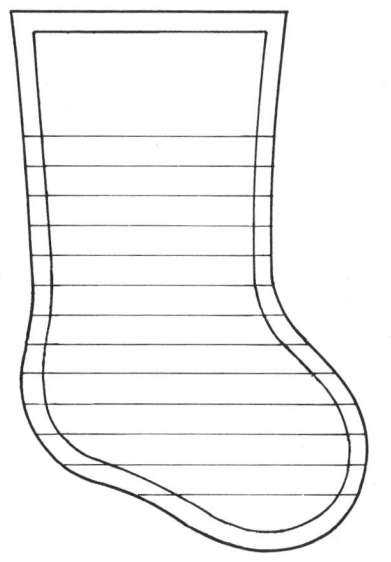

Fig 1 Pencil guide lines drawn on the backing fabric

down the stockings to act as a guide when stitching the fabric strips (Fig 1). Draw the lines parallel to the top edge of the stocking with the first line 9.5cm (3¾in) down from the top edge.

SEWING THE STRIPS TO THE BACKING

Make sure that the fabric strips are parallel to the lines drawn on the backing fabric. The strips must extend into the seam allowance on the backing fabric. Machine the strips 6mm (¼in) from the edge using the presser foot as a guide.

Begin the patchwork at the bottom of the stocking. Place the first strip, right side up, on the backing fabric. Pin and baste to the backing fabric (Fig 2).

Place the second strip on top of the first, right sides together. This strip needs to be longer than the first because the stocking gets wider at this point. With the top edges of the strips matching, pin through all the layers

116

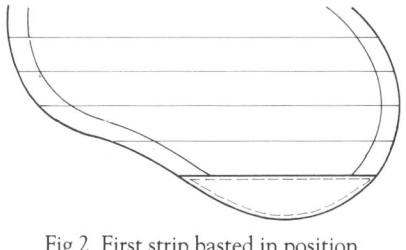

Fig 2 First strip basted in position

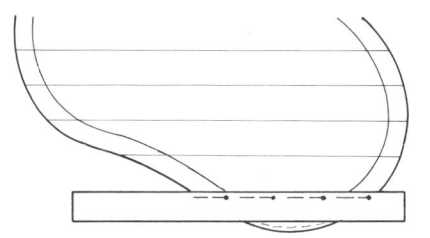

Fig 3 Second strip pinned in position

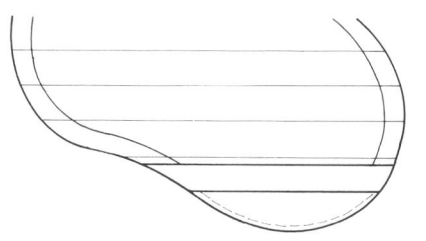

Fig 4 Second strip pressed to the right side

6mm (¼in) from the top edge (Fig 3). Fold the strip to the right side to check that it is long enough before machining the seam. Press the strip to the right side (Fig 4).

Continue adding strips, mixing the fabrics and varying the widths, until you reach the top drawn line. Add a strip of fabric 12cm (4¾in) wide to form the cuff. Press the cuff to the right side and baste the top and side edges to the backing fabric.

Make the stocking back in the same way. (If you are short of time, use a piece of plain fabric for the stocking back.)

Note Alternative method of working the patchwork: Work a piece of patchwork 76 x 56cm (30 x 22in). Cut strips of fabric 76cm (30in) long and stitch to the backing fabric following the instructions above. Draw round the template twice on the back of the patchwork, reversing the template to make a pair. Add a 12mm (½in) seam allowance all round. Cut out both pieces and continue with 'Decorating the Patchwork'. This method of making the stocking is quicker but a lot of fabric is wasted.

DECORATING THE PATCHWORK

Work a row of decorative machine stitching along some of the strips using cream or gold machine thread. Stitch a piece of lace across each side of the stocking just below the cuffs. Stitch 2 or 3 more pieces of lace at intervals down the stocking.

LINING THE STOCKING

Working from the back, where you can still see the stitching line, zigzag all round the stocking just inside the seam allowance.

Draw round the template twice on the wrong side of the lining fabric, reversing the pattern to make a pair. Add a 12mm (½in) seam allowance all round.

Line the stocking, following the instructions for the hessian stocking (see p113). Before turning the stocking to the right side, clip the curves on the patchwork stocking and on the lining.

Cut a piece of ribbon 20cm (8in) long to make a hanging loop. Fold in half and turn the ends under to neaten. Stitch the loop securely to the inside top of the back seam.

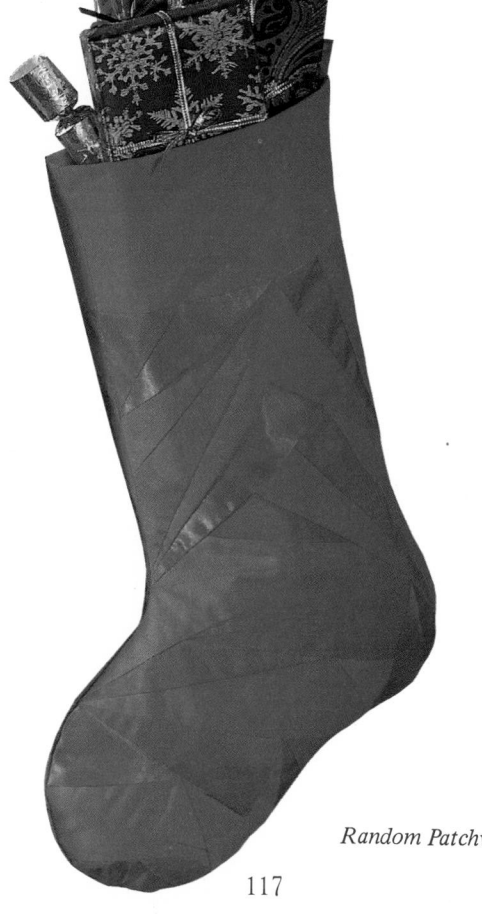

Random Patchwork Stocking (see p110)

117

Festive Trees

THREE
SIMPLE TREES

These three little trees will make an attractive table centre decoration. Each is made from fabrics which are bonded together. The edges are zigzagged on the machine; the two sections are stitched together, then opened out to make the three trees stand up.

•

APPROXIMATE HEIGHT

25cm (10in); 23cm (9in); 21cm (8in)

•

MATERIALS

30cm (½yd) red seasonal cotton fabric

30cm (½yd) green seasonal cotton fabric

30cm (½yd) white non-woven pelmet stiffener (eg pelmet or craft quality Vilene)

60cm (¾yd) fusible web (eg Bondaweb)

Red sewing cotton

Red felt-tip pen

Thin card and tracing paper for templates

•

Half patterns are given for the trees. Fold a piece of tracing paper in two. Open it out and position the fold over the fold line on the pattern and trace. Fold the tracing paper again and trace through the other half of the tree. To make the templates see Techniques and Stitches, p143.

Each tree has 2 sections. These are cut out of a rectangle made up from 2 pieces of fabric, one red, one green.

These are fused with fusible web to each side of the pelmet stiffener.

MAKING THE TREES

For the large tree cut a piece of pelmet stiffener 28 x 24cm (11 x 10in). Cut 1 piece each of green and red fabric the same size. Cut 2 pieces of fusible web the same size.

Fuse the green fabric to one side of the pelmet stiffener using the fusible web (follow the manufacturer's instructions). Fuse the red fabric to the other side of the pelmet stiffener. Press well.

Draw twice round the largest template on one side of the fabric with a fabric marking pen or pencil, positioning one beside the other.

Cut out both sections carefully along the line with sharp scissors. Colour the cut edges with a felt-tip pen.

Thread the machine with red thread.

Set the machine to a small zigzag stitch (practise on an offcut of material first to find a suitable stitch).

Machine round the edge of both halves of the tree.

Mark the centre line on a red side. Put the 2 halves together with the 2 green sides facing each other.

Set the machine to a tiny zigzag stitch and machine the 2 pieces together down the marked line, running back over a few stitches at the start and finish to secure. Trim off the threads.

Now fold the red sides together along the zigzagged line to reveal the green side. Machine again down the central seam (this helps the tree to stand squarely on a flat surface).

The fabric rectangles for the 2 other trees are: 25 x 24cm (10 x 10in) and 23 x 24cm (9 x 10in).

Zigzagging with the red surface exposed

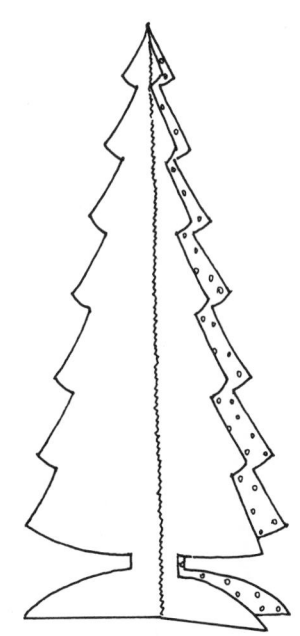

Zigzagging with the green surface exposed

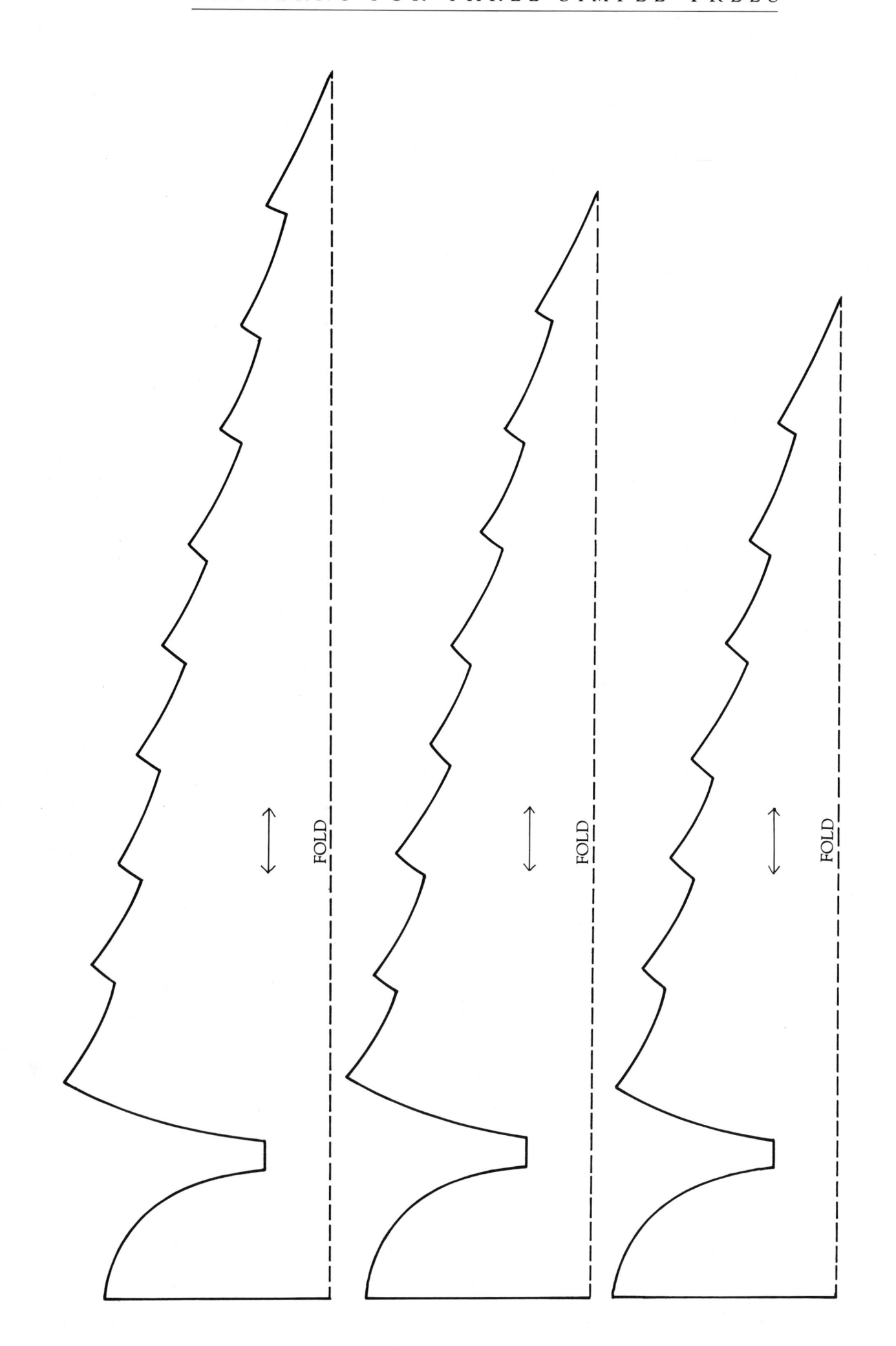

FOLD

FOLD

FOLD

PARTRIDGE IN A PEAR TREE

The partridge in a pear tree has long been a source of inspiration for Christmas card designers. Here it is represented in three-dimensional form to grace a mantelpiece or sideboard. Choose soft-coloured silks to create a very special decoration. Several techniques are used, including soft sculpture, needlelace and wrapping.

•

APPROXIMATE SIZE

TREE HEIGHT 56cm (22in)
PARTRIDGE 10 x15cm (4 x 6in)
PEAR 10cm (4in)

•

MATERIALS

PVA adhesive

Gold spray paint

Polyester toy stuffing

Tracing paper and thin card for templates

TREE

Wire cutters

Strong wire approximately 2mm (1/10in) diameter

OR small natural branch

Twilley's bronze Goldfingering
OR brown yarn and gold thread

Kitchen foil
OR small plastic bag

Double-sided adhesive tape

12cm (4½in) diameter plant pot

Plaster of Paris

Gravel (optional)

PARTRIDGE

Approximately 20 x 60cm (8 x 24in) soft orange or tan silk

Matching machine thread

Gold thread

2 bronze cup sequins (eyes)

Small gold cup sequins

PEARS AND LEAVES

30 x 122cm (12 x 48in) soft green silk

Matching machine thread

Small gold star sequins

Gold embroidery thread

Gold machine thread

Fusible web (eg Bondaweb)

•

MAKING THE TREE

A small natural branch of a tree could be used instead of the wrapped wire tree. Try to find one in which the partridge can perch. Lightly spray the branch with gold paint (see instructions below for finishing).

Cut a piece of stiff wire about 50cm (20in) long. Stick a small piece of double-sided tape round the end of the wire to hold the wrapping yarn in place temporarily. A little adhesive is added later to stop the yarn from slipping off the end of the wire.

Lay the wrapping yarn along the wire so that the end of the yarn is about 6cm (2½in) from the end of the wire. Start wrapping over the double-sided tape right at the end of the wire (Fig 1). Wrap tightly and smoothly, making sure that no wire shows.

As you wrap, lay extra pieces of yarn along the wire and wrap round those as well so that the branch gradually gets thicker. Continue wrapping until about 12cm (5in) of wire has been covered. Place a piece of sticky tape over the yarn and wire to prevent the yarn from unravelling and put the wire on one side. Cut a second piece of wire about 50cm (20in) long and wrap that in the same way until about 10cm (4in) of wire has been covered. Bind the 2 wires together for about 7cm (2¾in) before adding a third wrapped wire.

Bind the 3 wires together with extra lengths of yarn, if necessary, to make the trunk thicker (Fig 2a). Make a small forked branch with 2 pieces of wire about 35cm (14in) long. Wrap the end of 1 piece of wire for about 6cm (2½in) and the other piece for about 9cm (3½in). Bind the 2 wires together, then bind them to the trunk. This forked branch makes a perch for the partridge (Fig 2b).

Continue wrapping and adding branches until the tree is the required shape and size (Fig 2c). Leave about 7.5cm (3in) of the wire at the base of trunk uncovered. Put a little adhesive

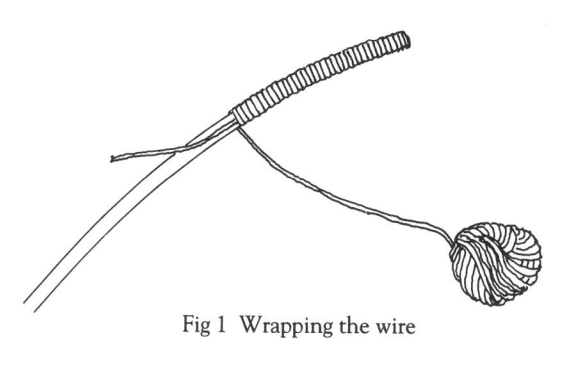

Fig 1 Wrapping the wire

PATTERNS FOR PARTRIDGE IN A PEAR TREE

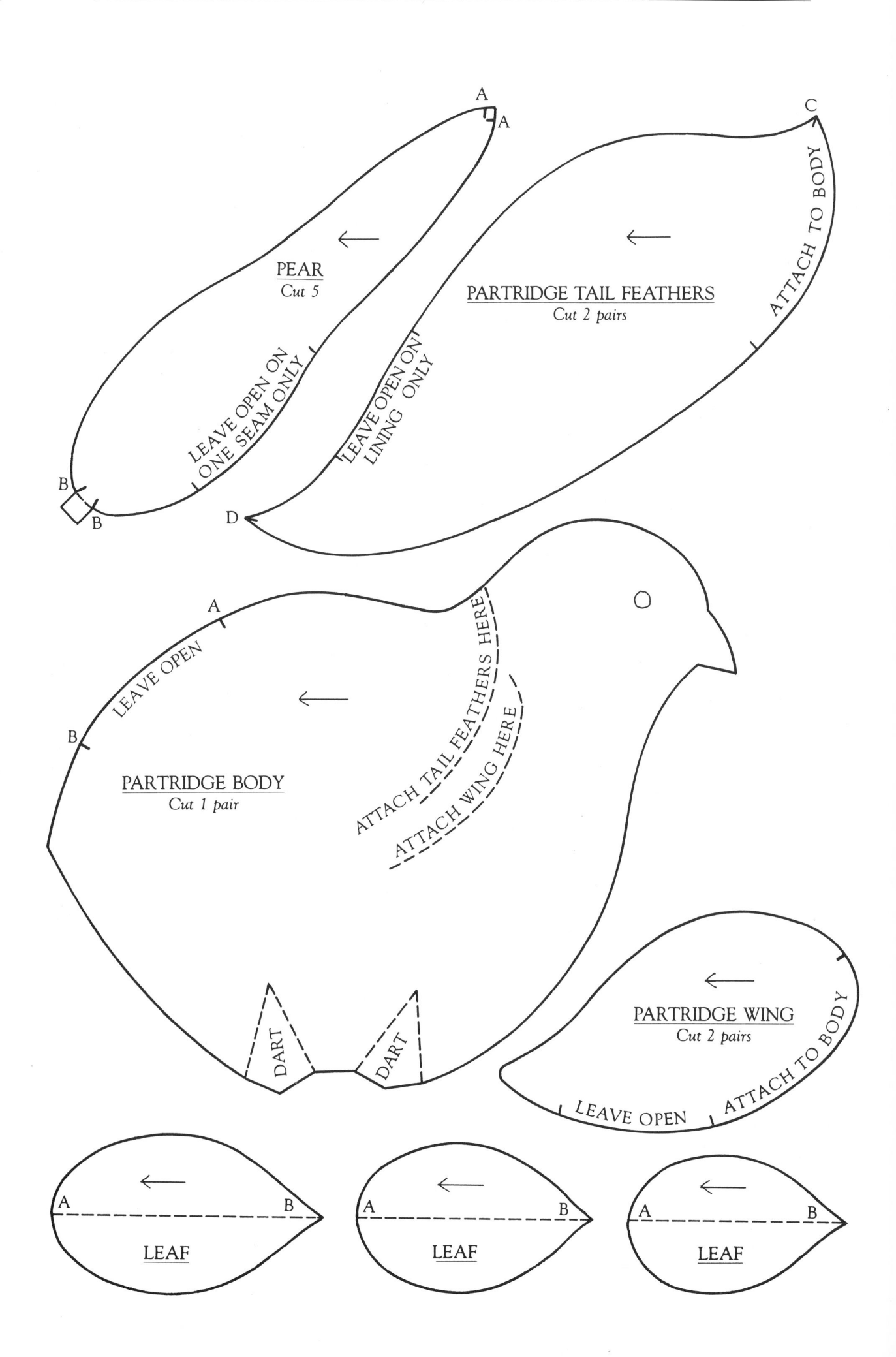

PEAR
Cut 5

PARTRIDGE TAIL FEATHERS
Cut 2 pairs

LEAVE OPEN ON ONE SEAM ONLY

LEAVE OPEN ON LINING ONLY

ATTACH TO BODY

PARTRIDGE BODY
Cut 1 pair

LEAVE OPEN

ATTACH TAIL FEATHERS HERE

ATTACH WING HERE

DART

DART

PARTRIDGE WING
Cut 2 pairs

LEAVE OPEN

ATTACH TO BODY

LEAF

LEAF

LEAF

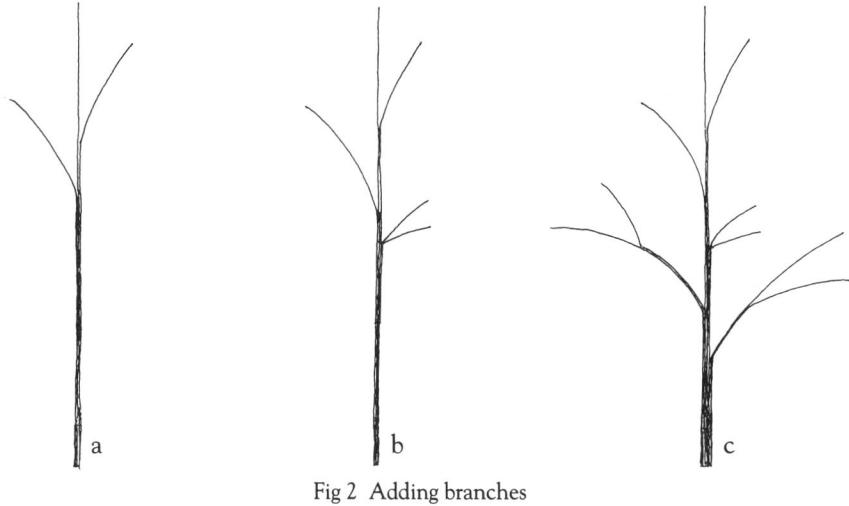

Fig 2 Adding branches

on the last few threads at the ends of the branches to prevent them from slipping off. Cut the wires level at the base and splay them out to give a firm anchorage in the pot.

Spray the outside of the plant pot with gold paint. Allow to dry, then line the inside of the pot with kitchen foil or a small plastic bag. Mix enough plaster of Paris to fill the pot, adding water until it is the consistency of thick cream. Stand the tree or natural branch in the pot and pour in the plaster of Paris. Smooth the top and leave to dry completely. Spread a thick layer of adhesive on the surface of the plaster and cover with a layer of gravel. This is optional but it does give an interesting texture. When dry, very lightly spray the gravel and the tree with gold paint.

MAKING THE PARTRIDGE

Use matching thread and a small machine stitch for all seams. Basting and ladder stitch should also be worked in matching thread. Trace the patterns and make templates (see Techniques and Stitches, p143). Draw round templates on the wrong side of the fabric reversing the templates to make pairs. This is the stitching line. Add a 12mm (½in) seam allowance all round. Cut out 1 pair of bodies, 2 pairs of wings and 2 pairs of tail 'feathers'.

Sew the darts in the bird bodies. Place 2 body pieces, right sides together, and pin round the edge, carefully matching the stitching lines. Keep looking at the back to make sure

that the pins are in the correct position. Baste together on the stitching line with a small running stitch. Machine round the body from A to B.

Trim the seam allowance to about 3mm (⅛in), leaving 6mm (¼in) on each side of the opening. Carefully spread a thin line of adhesive along the cut edge. This is important because it prevents the seam from splitting when the partridge is stuffed. If a wider seam allowance is left, it is difficult to get really smooth seams and a good shape to the bird. Work a row of tiny running stitches along the seam line on each side of the opening. This will help you to stitch in the correct place when ladder stitching the opening after stuffing.

Turn the partridge right side out and stuff with small pieces of polyester stuffing. Stuff firmly, trying to avoid lumps on the surface of the silk. Ladder stitch the opening (see Techniques and Stitches, p142).

MAKING THE WINGS

Place a pair of wings right sides together and pin and baste all round. Machine round the wing on the stitching line, leaving an opening for turning. Trim the seam and turn right side out. Ladder stitch the opening. Make a second wing in the same way.

MAKING THE TAIL FEATHERS

With right sides together, pin and machine one pair of tail feathers from

C to D, carefully matching the stitching lines. Repeat for the lining pair, leaving an opening for turning as shown on the pattern. Trim the seam allowance to 6mm (¼in). Place the pairs of tail feathers right sides together and carefully pin and baste them all round, matching the stitching lines. Machine all round. Trim the seam and turn right side out. Ladder stitch the opening.

DECORATING THE PARTRIDGE

Use gold thread to work 2 rows of feather stitch (see Techniques and Stitches, p142) round the neck of the bird and 1 row round each of the wings and the tail feathers. Remember to reverse one of the wings so that you have a pair. Sew small gold sequins among the feather stitches and bronze sequins in position for the eyes.

Slip stitch the tail feathers and wings in position as shown on the pattern.

MAKING THE PEARS

Use matching thread and a small machine stitch for all seams. Basting and ladder stitch should also be worked in matching thread.

Trace the pattern and make a template. Match the arrow to the grain of the fabric. This is important because maximum stretch is needed round the pear to give a pleasing shape. Draw round the template on the wrong side of the fabric. This is the stitching line. Add a 6mm (¼in) seam allowance all round. Cut out 5 pieces. With right sides together, carefully pin 2 pieces on the stitching line, matching points A and B. Keep looking at the back to make sure that the pins are in the correct place. Baste on the stitching line using a small running stitch. Machine the seam from A to B. Carefully pin, baste and machine the other 3 pieces together in the same way. Join the 2 sections, right sides together, leaving an opening for turning in the last seam.

Cut a 6cm (2½in) square of silk and spread a little adhesive thinly all over the wrong side. Roll the square diagonally to form a stalk (Fig 3). Trim the ends so that the stalk is about 6cm (2½in) long. Push the

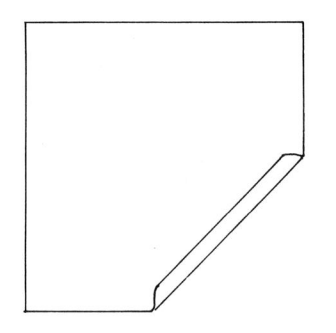

Fig 3 Making the stalk

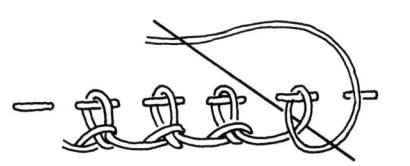

Fig 4 Knotted detached buttonhole stitch

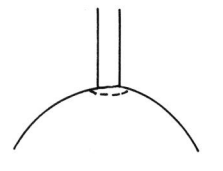

Fig 5 Running stitch round
top of pear

MAKING THE LEAVES

Make approximately 40 leaves in mixed sizes, mainly small and medium with a few large ones. Trace the patterns and make templates.

The leaves are made from 2 layers of silk fused together with fusible web. Cut 2 pieces of silk and one piece of fusible web 30 x 38cm (12 x 15in). Iron the fusible web onto the wrong side of one piece of silk. Remove the paper backing and place on top of the second piece of silk, wrong sides together. Press with a dry iron and damp cloth. Use a fine pencil to draw round the templates on the silk.

Use fine metallic gold machine thread in the needle and spool of your machine. Pull the ends of the threads until they are about 15cm (6in) long. (The ends of all the machine threads will be used to sew the leaves to the tree.) Starting at the base of the leaf A, work a row of straight machine stitch down the centre to the tip B. Work a narrow zigzag stitch all round the leaf on the pencil line and then another row of straight stitch on top of the first, ending at A. Cut the ends of the thread level with the starting threads.

Carefully cut out the leaves close to the zigzag stitches. Fold the leaves down the centre stitching to emphasise the veins. Try to curve the leaves a little by placing them on the edge of the ironing-board and pressing with a warm iron. Spray the leaves lightly with gold paint on the top surface only.

ASSEMBLING THE TREE

Bend and twist the tree, if necessary, to make an attractive, interesting shape. Pin the leaves and pears to the branches and put the partridge on the perch. Adjust the leaves and pears until you are happy with the arrangement, then sew them on. The leaves and pears will have to be glued in place if you use a natural branch of a tree.

stalk through the gap at point A (at the top of the pear) so that the end just pokes through to the wrong side. Hand stitch the stalk in place with a few small neat stitches. Make quite sure that the gap is closed completely.

Trim the seams to about 3mm (⅛in), leaving 6mm (¼in) on each side of the opening. Carefully spread a very thin line of adhesive along the cut edge. This is important because it prevents the seam from splitting when the pear is stuffed. Work a row of tiny running stitches along the seam line on both sides of the opening. This will help you to stitch in the correct place when ladder stitching the opening.

Turn the pear right side out. Make sure that the unstitched area at the base of the pear is pushed to the right side. This forms the calyx. Work a row of small gathering stitches along the stitching line round the base of the pear B - B. Pull the gathers up tight and fasten off securely.

Stuff the pear, inserting small amounts of stuffing at a time. Try to achieve a really smooth surface and a nice round shape. Ladder stitch the opening following the row of running stitches on the stitching line.

DECORATING THE PEAR

The pear is covered with needlelace (detached, knotted buttonhole stitch (Fig 4) worked in a random way). No attempt is made to keep the stitches an even size.

Using gold thread, begin by working a row of small running stitches round the top of the pear, just below where the stalk joins the pear (Fig 5). The first row of knotted buttonhole stitch is worked into the running stitches. The next and following rows are worked into the loops of the previous rows. Vary the size of the stitches by occasionally missing a loop or working 2 or more stitches into the same loop to make an interesting pattern of spaces. As the circumference of the pear increases, you may find that you need to take a small stitch into the pear to hold the needlelace in place. This will not show if a tiny stitch is worked over a knot. Continue until the pear is covered with needlelace. Stitch small gold star sequins in some of the larger spaces (Fig 6).

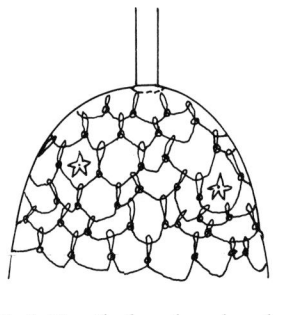

Fig 6 Detail of random detached buttonhole stitch

BIRD IN FLOWER TREE

This beautiful silk bird is made to nest in a tree of flowers and makes a really lovely decoration to put on a side-table or mantelpiece. Choosing a silk for the bird, to complement the colour of the dried flowers you have chosen.

•

APPROXIMATE HEIGHT

50cm (20in)

•

MATERIALS
TREE

7cm (2¾in) diameter florist's foam ball for dried flowers

10cm (4in) diameter clean flowerpot

Plaster of Paris

36cm (14in) of 1cm (³⁄₈in) dowel

Dried flowers

Dried reindeer moss

Gold and silver spray paint

Fir cones or glass baubles (optional)

BIRD

20cm (8in) shot pale coloured silk

Matching machine thread

Large bronze star sequins

Small gold star sequins

Small cup sequins

Small gold glass beads

Thin gold beading wire and wire-cutters

Gold machine thread

Polyester stuffing

PVA adhesive

Thin card and tracing paper for templates

MAKING THE TREE

Begin by making a hole through the centre of the foam ball with a fine knitting-needle. Insert a larger needle to produce a larger hole. The finished hole must be big enough to take the dowel and yet be a tight fit.

Taper the end of the dowel and insert it right through the ball.

Add enough water to some plaster of Paris to make a thick cream. Fill the flowerpot to 2cm (1in) below the rim. When it is on the point of setting, push the dowel end into the centre of the pot, making sure it is vertical.

When the plaster of Paris is dry, spray the dowel and pot with gold and silver paint. A mottled effect is attractive with one layer showing a little below the other. Cover the plaster of Paris with some reindeer moss; this can also be sprayed with paint.

Cut dried flowers into lengths of about 10cm (4in) and begin pushing them into the ball. The ball will use a lot of flowers to produce a tight round flower tree. Leave the top of the ball free of flowers to form a nest for the bird to sit in. Some tiny fir cones can be wired and added at intervals, as can very small glass baubles.

MAKING THE BIRD

Use a matching thread and a small machine stitch for all seams. Basting and ladder stitches should also be worked in a matching thread.

Trace the pattern for the bird body and wing and make templates (see Techniques and Stitches, p143).

Draw round the body template on the wrong side of the fabric twice, reversing the template to make a pair. Cut out, leaving a 6mm (¼in) seam allowance.

Machine the darts in the bird bodies. Baste the turning at the tail openings between A and B to the wrong side. Pin the body pieces, right sides together, carefully matching the stitching lines. Baste along the stitching line with small stitches and then machine round the body from A to B.

Trim the seam to 3mm (⅛in) and carefully spread a thin line of adhesive along the cut edge. This is important because it prevents the seam from splitting when the bird is stuffed.

Turn the bird right side out, and stuff from the tail opening with small pieces of stuffing. Stuff firmly, trying to avoid lumps on the surface of the silk.

Turn the tail opening to bring seam A and B together and pin.

MAKING THE WINGS

On the wrong side of the fabric, draw round the template 4 times to produce 2 pairs for each wing (watch the direction of the grain). Cut out, leaving a 6mm (¼in) seam allowance. Pin and baste 2 wing pieces, right sides together. Machine round the wing on the stitching line, leaving an opening for turning. Trim the seams and turn right side out. Ladder stitch the opening (see Techniques and Stitches, p142).

Make a second wing in the same way.

Decorate the wings on one side with a large star sequin motif (Fig 1) and 3 cup sequins (Fig 2). Use the

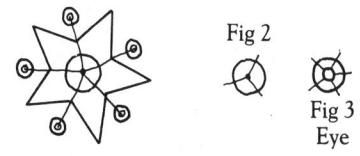

Fig 2

Fig 3
Eye

Fig 1 Large star motif

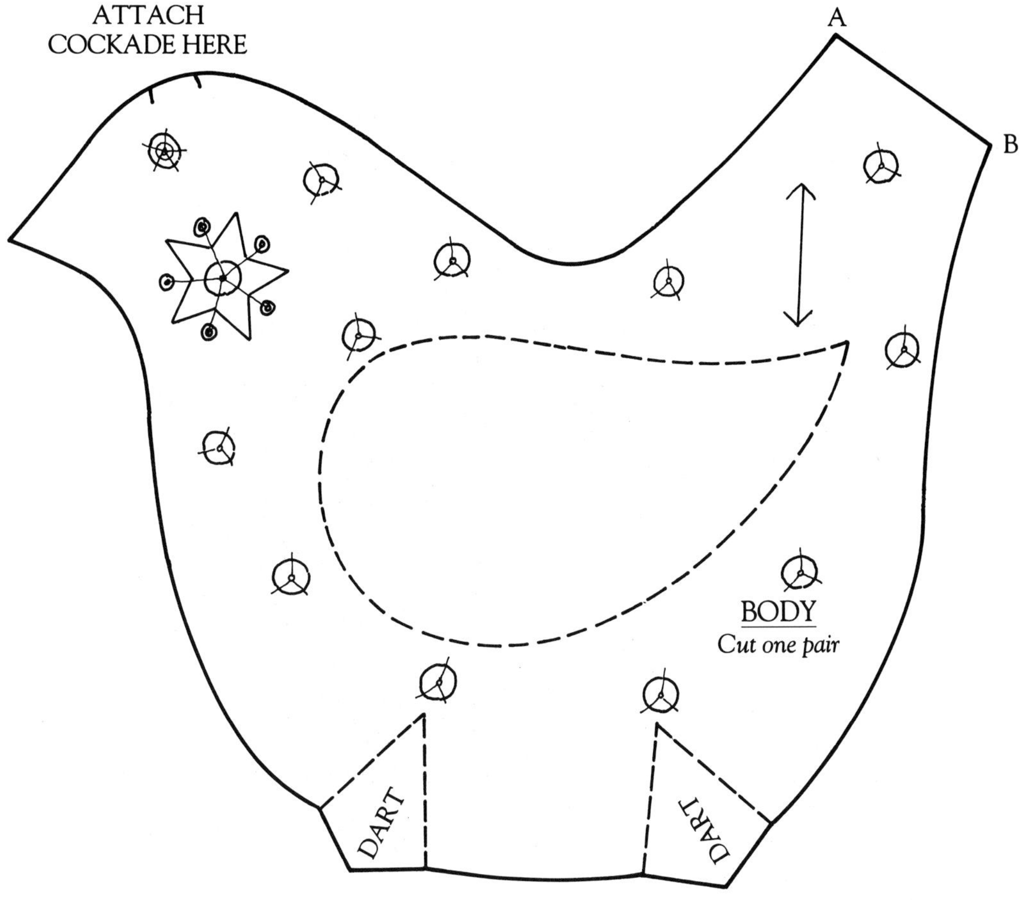

ATTACH
COCKADE HERE

A

B

BODY
Cut one pair

DART

DART

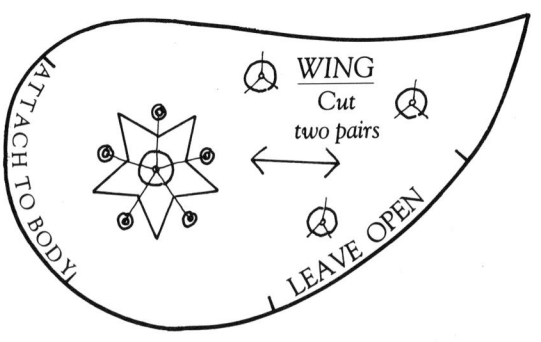

ATTACH TO BODY

WING
Cut
two pairs

LEAVE OPEN

pattern as a guide and stitch the sequins with gold machine thread.

Oversew a piece of wire down the centre of the underside of each wing.

Decorate the bird in the same way using the pattern as a guide (see Fig 3 for the eye). Slip stitch the wings onto the bird as indicated on the wing pattern.

MAKING THE COCKADE

The cockade has a frayed fringe along the top, so if you are using shot silk, decide whether you prefer the warp or weft threads to show in the fringe. The same threads will make a feature in the tail feathers.

Cut a rectangle of silk 3.5 x 5.5cm (1⅜ x 2¼in) (Fig 4). Draw the threads out for the fringe to a depth of 15mm (⅝in). Fold under a 3mm (⅛in) turning along the lower edge and press. Fold the same allowance along the sides. Fold the rectangle in two and slip stitch the sides together. Gather the lower edge with tiny running stitches. Pull tight and fasten off securely.

The cockade is decorated with small star sequins threaded and twisted onto each end of lengths of wire. Cut 5 lengths 7.5cm (3in) long and twist a sequin onto both ends of each (see Decorated Walnuts, p17). Tie the wires together in the middle and, with the same thread, attach them under the gathers of the cockade. Bend them up and make them fan out along either side of the cockade (Fig 5).

Slip stitch the finished cockade along both sides to the bird's head.

MAKING THE TAIL

The tail is made of strips of silk with a wire machine zigzagged down the centre. The silk is frayed on either side of the wire. Some beaded wires are added to the feathers. A cluster of feathers and wires is stitched together and inserted into the tail opening.

For the tail feathers, cut a rectangle of silk 13 x 14cm (5 x 5½in). Your chosen weave for the fringing must go across the rectangle. There are 9 feathers, so each is approximately 15mm (⅝in) wide. On the back of the fabric draw 9 evenly spaced lines and down these couch gold wires using

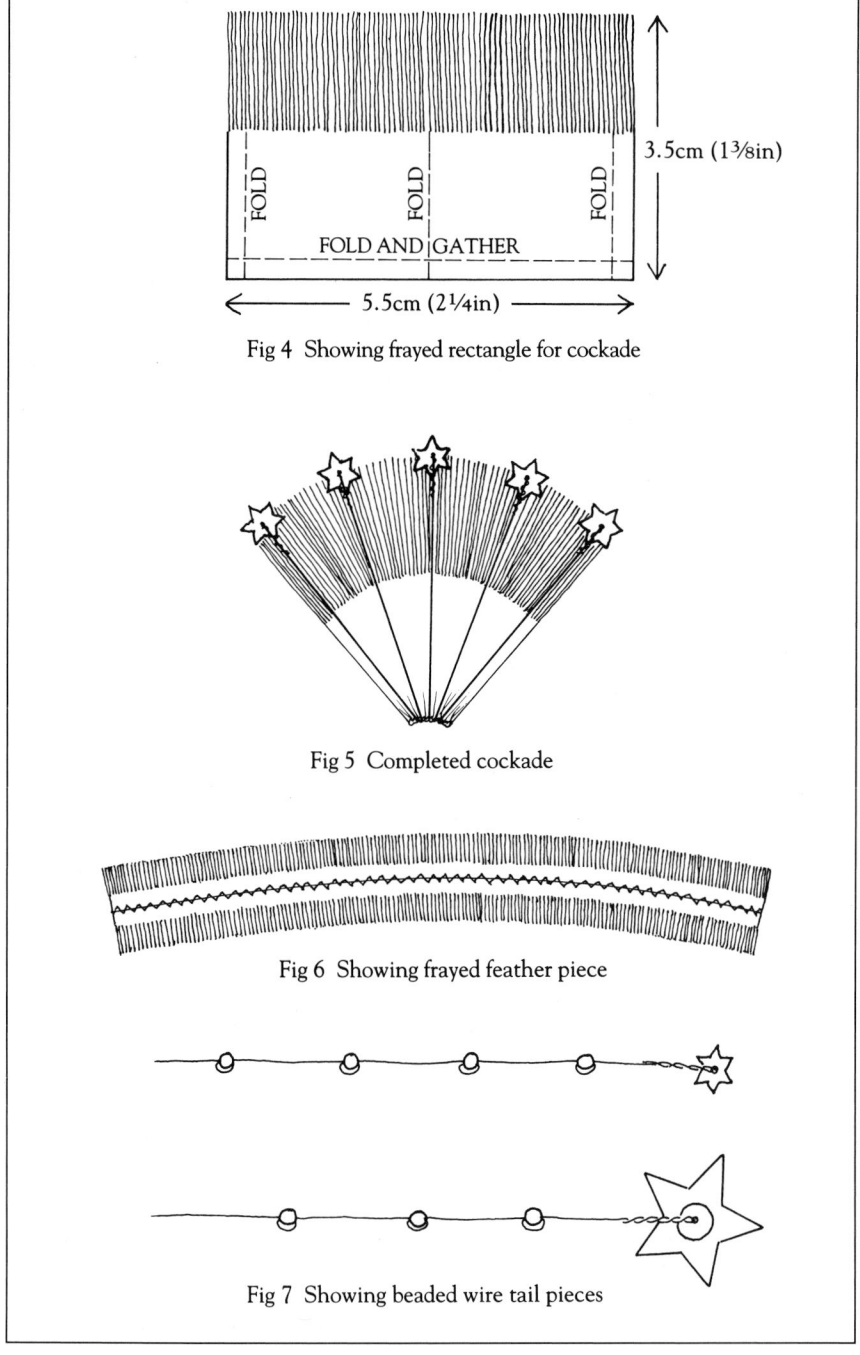

Fig 4 Showing frayed rectangle for cockade

3.5cm (1⅜in)

FOLD AND GATHER

5.5cm (2¼in)

Fig 5 Completed cockade

Fig 6 Showing frayed feather piece

Fig 7 Showing beaded wire tail pieces

a small zigzag stitch and gold metallic machine thread. A good tip is to leave a few millimetres of wire free at both ends which can be bent back over the stitching to prevent the wires from pulling out.

Cut the rectangle into strips on either side of the wires and pull out threads to make the fringes (Fig 6).

Cut 8 lengths of wire 18cm (7in) long and onto these thread 3 or 4 gold glass beads at intervals (see Decorated Walnuts, p17). At one end of each wire thread and twist either a large

star sequin with a cupped sequin on top or a small gold star sequin (Fig 7).

Gather the tail pieces and wires together and stitch them firmly at one end, making a width of about 2.5cm (1in) to fit neatly into the tail opening.

Place the tail into the opening of the bird, pin and slip stitch firmly in place.

Arch the tail feathers and wires to look attractive. Bend the wings into a nice curve and position the bird in the top of the tree.

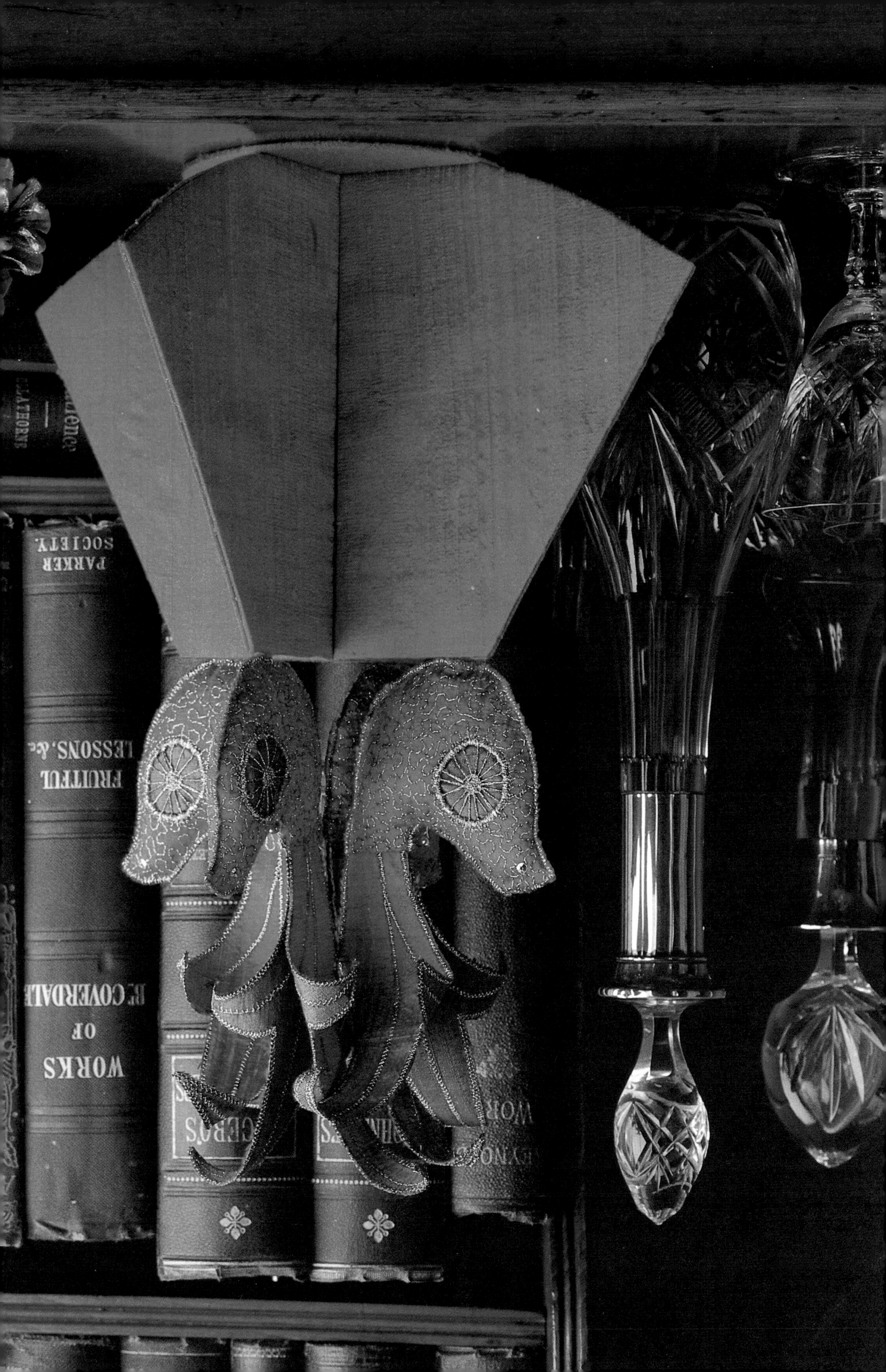
PARKER SOCIETY.
FRUITFUL LESSONS, &c.
WORKS OF Bp. COVERDALE

SILK BIRD TREE

This little collection of machine-embroidered birds is made in a festive coloured silk which is not particularly associated with Christmas, so they could stand on a mantelpiece or table to celebrate any special occasion. Of course, there is no reason why you should not make them in seasonal colours.

·

APPROXIMATE HEIGHT

30cm (12in)

·

MATERIALS

½m (½yd) pink silk

20cm (8in) contrast silk

½m (½yd) lightweight iron-on fabric stiffener (eg Vilene)

½m (½yd) fusible web (eg Bondaweb)

Variegated metallic machine thread

Craft wire

Thin beading or florist's wire

Wire-cutters

4 small beads

8 small sequins

Polyester stuffing

20cm (8in) embroidery hoop

PVA adhesive

Thin card and tracing paper for templates

Trace the patterns for the birds, tail and tree and make templates (see Techniques and Stitches, p143).

MAKING THE BIRDS

The bird bodies are free machine embroidered and have a cutwork wheel on both sides (see general instructions for free machine embroidery, p140). Prepare 4 body sections at a time to be worked in a 20cm (8in) embroidery hoop. Cut a square of pink silk and iron-on fabric stiffener 26cm (10in). Iron the fabric stiffener onto one side of the silk. On the right side draw round the template 4 times, reversing it to make 2 pairs of body pieces. Draw the circles for machine cutwork. Leave space for seam allowance between each section. Place the fabric in an embroidery hoop. Set the machine for free machine embroidery and thread with metallic thread. Work vermicelli stitch (Fig 1) on each body section, keeping the stitching within the drawn margins. Machine round the cutwork circles, then cut away the fabric up to the stitched lines and work the lace fillings (see p141).

Remove the work from the hoop and cut out the birds, leaving a 6mm

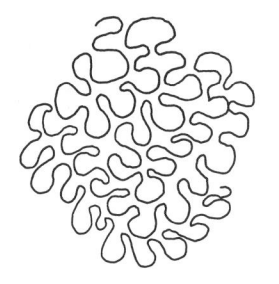

Fig 1 Vermicelli stitch

(¼in) allowance.

Cut 4 small squares of contrast silk and hand stitch them in place behind the cutwork wheels against the zigzagged edge.

The birds are fixed onto the tree by wires inserted through them and these are then glued in place behind fabric-covered card. To prepare the wires, cut 4 lengths of craft wire 16cm (6½in). Thread a bead onto the centre of each, fold the wires in two and give a twist to the bead to hold it firmly onto the wire (see Bird Tree Hanging, p74).

Fold and press 6mm (¼in) turnings to the wrong side along the tail seams. Pin and baste 2 bird pieces together, wrong sides facing, along the marked lines. Mitre the allowance at B and C (Fig 2). Set the machine for normal

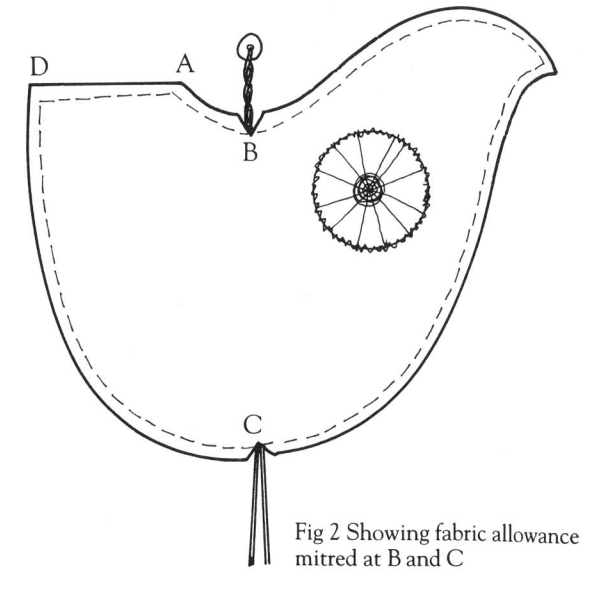

Fig 2 Showing fabric allowance mitred at B and C

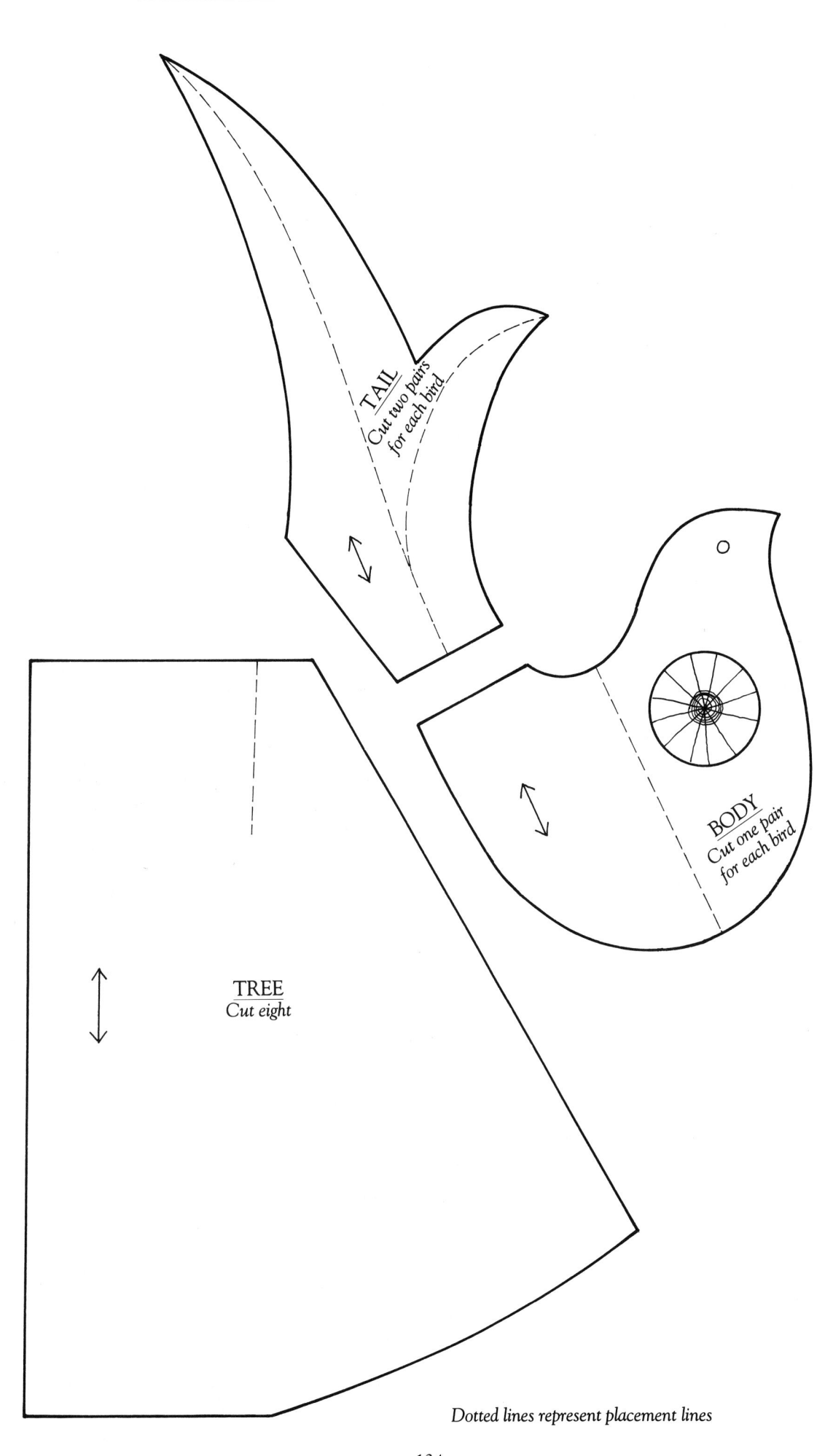

TAIL
Cut two pairs
for each bird

BODY
Cut one pair
for each bird

TREE
Cut eight

Dotted lines represent placement lines

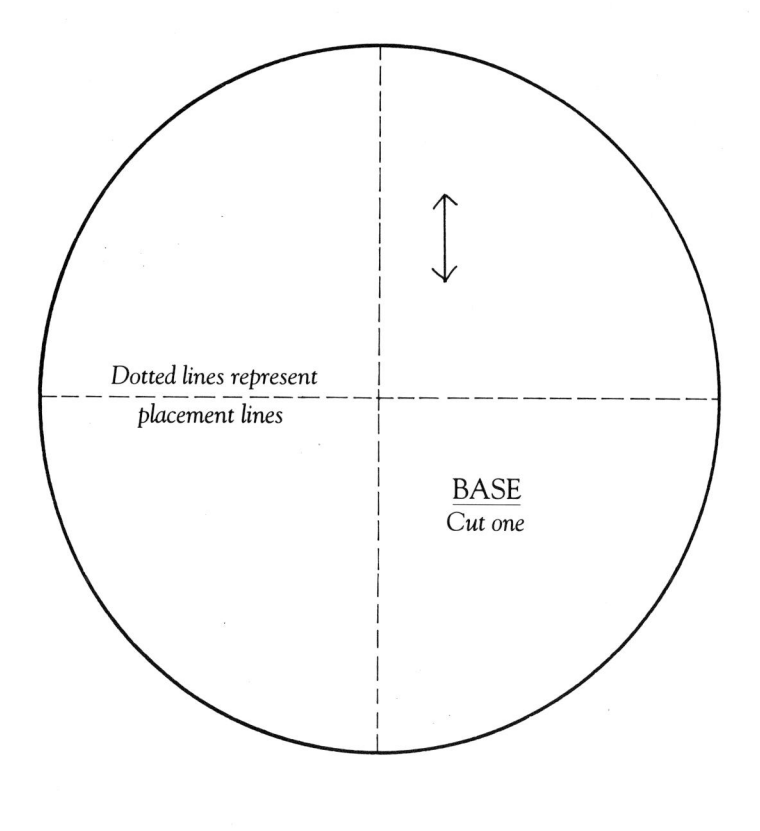

Dotted lines represent placement lines

BASE
Cut one

sewing and prepare to machine round the bird using a small straight stitch. Start at the tail opening point A, insert a wire at point B to come out at point C (leave the bead 6mm (¼in) up from the seam to make it easier to stitch). Free-wheel the machine over the wire and continue to stitch round to point D, free-wheeling the machine over the wire at point C. Secure the threads at the start and finish.

Cut away the fabric up to the stitching line and work round the bird again with a small close zigzag over the straight stitch (free-wheel the machine again over the wires, being careful not to catch them in the stitching). Pull the wire to bring the bead up against the stitching.

Stuff the bird with small pieces of stuffing. Do not overstuff – the bird should not be too firm. Sew a sequin in position for an eye on each side. Finish the second bird and make 2 more in the same way.

MAKING THE TAILS

Cut a square of pink silk, contrast silk and fusible web 28cm (11in). Fuse the silks together with the fusible web (see manufacturer's instructions). Draw round the tail template 4 times in one direction and 4 times in the other to make 4 pairs. Machine round the tails just inside the marked line using a small straight stitch, not including the base.

Cut 16 lengths of fine wire 13cm (5¼in). Use the tail pattern as a guide and stitch over the wires down the centre of the pink silk side with a small zigzag. Cut off the surplus with wire-cutters. Machine round again with a small close zigzag over the original stitching not including the base of the tails. Cut out the tails close to the stitching but leave a 6mm (¼in) allowance at the base. Hand stitch 2 tail pieces together at the base, contrast silk sides facing, and insert into the tail opening of the birds. Slip stitch each side of the tail to the folded edge of the opening.

MAKING THE TREE

Draw round the tree template on thin card 8 times and cut out. Draw the bird placement lines.

Fold a piece of tracing paper 14 x 24cm (5½ x 9½in) in two vertically. Position the long vertical edge of the tree template along the fold, draw round it and cut out to make a pattern. Pin the pattern onto a piece of pink silk and cut out, leaving a 15mm (⅝in) allowance all round.

Cut out 3 more tree pieces. Use the pattern and draw the top and bottom straight edges on the silk. Fold and press the seam allowance along the line to the wrong side.

Pin 2 pieces, wrong sides together. Repeat with the other 2 pieces. Place the 2 pinned sections together, draw the centre line on one side and machine down it, working back over a few stitches, at the start and finish, to secure. Trim the threads and remove the pins. Slot the cards in position inside the turnings of the 8 tree sections. The turnings are then glued down onto the card. Fold and glue the side allowance over the card. Glue the birds in position along the placement lines and leave to dry. Bring 2 cards together and glue. Repeat with the other 6 cards.

Cut out a circular card base, position on the silk and cut out leaving 15mm (⅝in) turnings which are glued over the back. Glue a circle of silk over the turnings to neaten the underside of the base. Mark the placement lines on the top side of the base and carefully glue the tree along them.

Curl the wired tails of the birds forward to make an attractive arched effect.

Techniques
and Stitches

BEADS AND SEQUINS

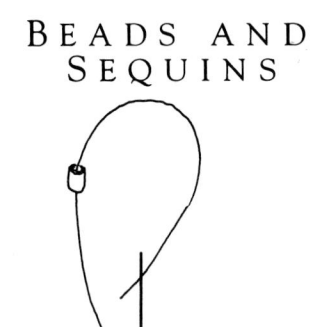

Sewing down a single bead

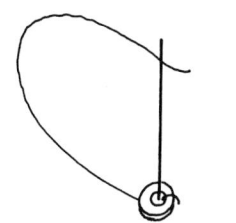

Sewing down a bead with its hole facing upwards

Holding down a sequin with stitches

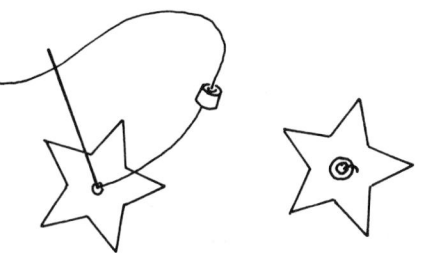

Holding down a sequin with a bead

CARD ENVELOPE

Having made your Christmas cards you will want an envelope tailor-made for each. If a quantity is needed, make a template to save time.

Take the card measurements and add an extra 6mm (¼in) to the length and width (Fig 1).

Make a plan on a piece of paper to estimate the overall size of paper required for the envelope.

Draw a rectangle the size of the finished envelope and plan the flaps. The side flaps should be not less than 25mm (1in). The bottom flap should

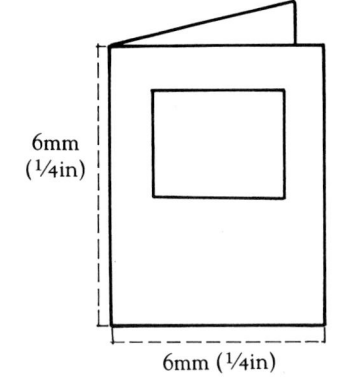

6mm (¼in)

6mm (¼in)

Fig 1 A card (not to scale) 14cm x 10cm (5½in x 4in) showing extra allowance added for envelope size

be three-quarters of the card's width plus 12mm (½in) for overlap; the top flap should be a quarter of the card's width plus 12mm (½in) for overlap (Fig 2).

Draw this shape onto your chosen paper. Taper the top and bottom flaps. Curve the side flaps using a coin as a guide. Cut out the envelope and score the dotted lines (Fig 2).

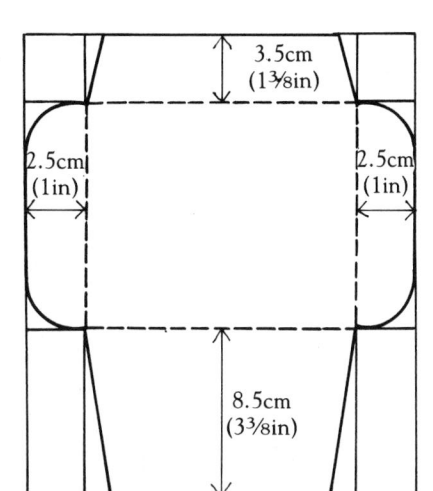

3.5cm (1⅜in)

2.5cm (1in)

2.5cm (1in)

8.5cm (3⅜in)

Fig 2 Layout for envelope

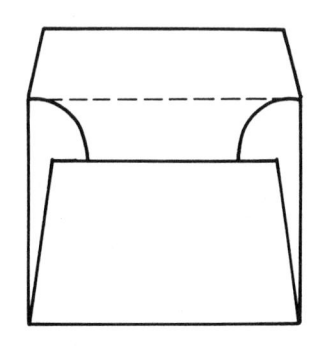

Fig 3 Finished envelope

Turn in the side flaps. Apply adhesive to the side edges of the bottom flap, turn it up and stick it to the side flaps. The envelope is now complete (Fig 3).

When you are ready to use the envelope, close it either with adhesive or double-sided adhesive tape along the top flap.

CARD MOUNTING

Cards which are embroidered or made with fabric are usually mounted behind a 'window' in the central section of a triple fold. The third section is folded and glued across the back of the needlework to make a neat finish inside the card.

MATERIALS

Thin coloured card

Craft knife or paper scissors

Metal ruler

Cutting mat

PVA adhesive or double-side adhesive tape

Sharp pencil

Set square

For each project in the card section, an exact pattern is given for the centre fold (Fig 1), which can be used as a guide when preparing the finished card. The two folds on either side are of equal size.

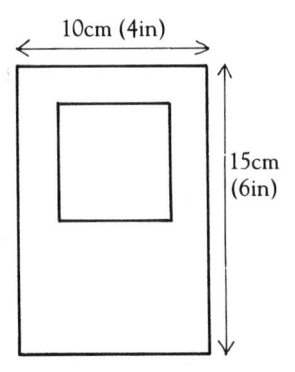

10cm (4in)

15cm (6in)

Fig 1 Pattern for card (not to scale)

PREPARING A WINDOW CARD

Take the measurements given for a project and work out on a piece of paper the exact size for the triple fold.

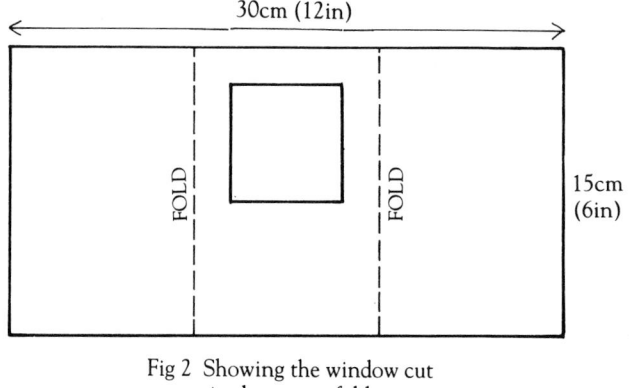

Fig 2 Showing the window cut
in the centre fold

The window is cut in the centre (Fig 2).

Start at one corner of your sheet of coloured card and measure and draw the triple fold using a sharp pencil. Use a set square to make exact right angles and be accurate with your measurements.

Cut the card with paper scissors or a craft knife. (If you are using a knife, always cut with a metal ruler and make sure that your blade is sharp.)

On the right side of the card score along the two dotted lines and fold (Fig 3).

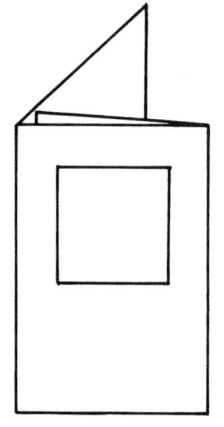

Fig 3 Finished card

On the vertical edge of the third fold cut off 2mm (⅛in). This makes it lie flat when it is folded back over the needlework.

Trim the needlework to fit just behind the window. Put a line of adhesive round the back of the opening and fix the work in place.

Put a line of adhesive round all 4 edges on the back of the third fold and press down over the back of the needlework.

An excellent alternative to adhesive is double-sided adhesive tape. Cut strips and attach them round the back of the window. Peel away the backing paper and press the needlework in place

Add more strips round the edges of the back of the centre fold and press the third fold down over the back of the needlework.

When a piece of stitchery is first mounted over a piece of thin card, a double fold is sufficient. The mounted work is glued in place onto the front of the folded card, using the given pattern as a positioning guide.

CROCHET ABBREVIATIONS

	UK	USA
ch	chain	chain
sl st	slip stitch	slip stitch
dc	double crochet	single crochet
htr	half treble crochet	half double crochet
tr	treble crochet	double crochet
dtr	double treble crochet	triple crochet
beg	beginning	
lp	loop	
rnd	round	
sp	space	

( ) Instructions written within brackets should be worked the number of times stated after the brackets eg (2 dc, 2 ch, 2 dc) 4 times, means 4 times in all.

* An asterisk indicates the beginning of instructions which have to be worked more than once eg *ch 6, 1 dtr in next 2 ch sp . . . , repeat from * 4 times, means the instructions are worked once then repeated 4 times, 5 times in all.

CROCHET STITCHES

Chain stitch (ch) Fig 1 Begin with a slip knot (Figs 1a and 1b). Yarn over hook and pull through loop on hook (new loop on hook).

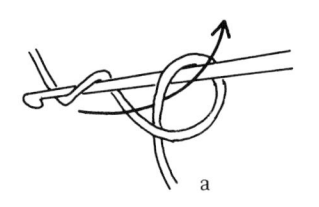

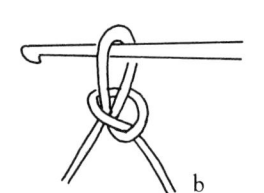

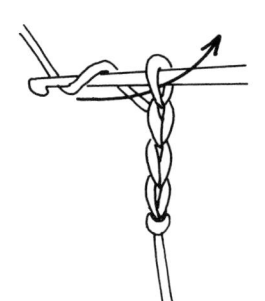

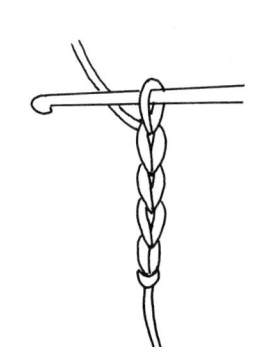

Fig 1 Slip knot and chain stitch

Fig 2 Slip stitch (sl st) Insert hook in stitch, yarn over hook and pull through stitch and loop on hook.

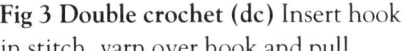

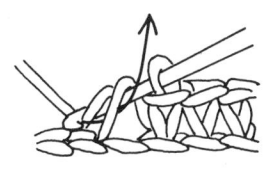

Fig 3 Double crochet (dc) Insert hook in stitch, yarn over hook and pull through stitch (2 loops on hook), yarn over hook and pull through both loops on hook.

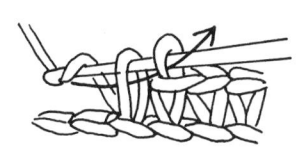

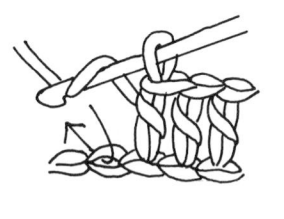

Fig 4 Half treble (htr) Yarn over hook, insert hook in stitch, yarn over hook and pull through stitch (3 loops on hook), yarn over hook and pull through all 3 loops on hook.

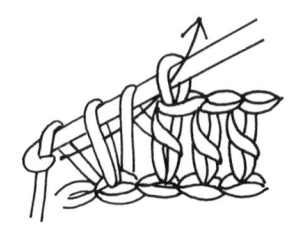

Fig 5 Treble (tr) Yarn over hook, insert hook in stitch, yarn over hook and pull through stitch (3 loops on hook), (yarn over hook and pull through 2 loops on hook) twice.

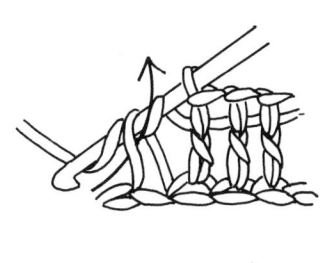

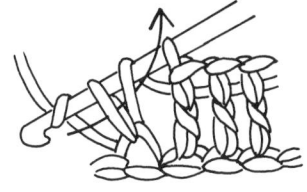

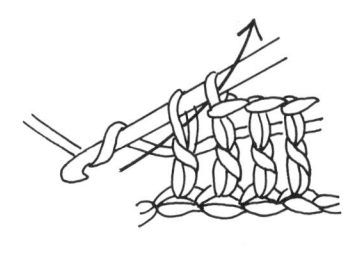

Fig 6 Double treble (dtr) Yarn over hook twice, insert hook in stitch, yarn over hook and pull through stitch (4 loops on hook), (yarn over hook and pull through 2 loops on hook) 3 times.

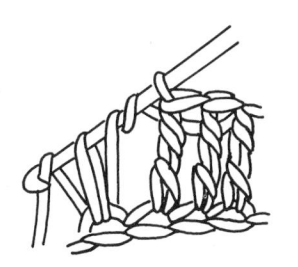

Fig 7 Beginning with a ring Chain 8, slip stitch in 1st chain to form a ring.

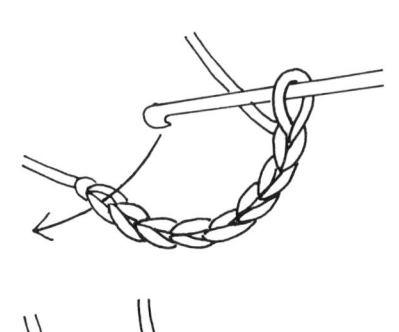

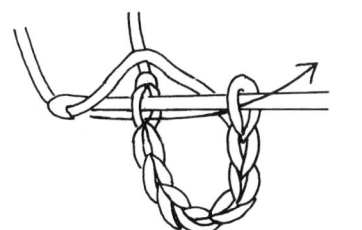

ENLARGING

The stocking pattern is the only one which is enlarged with the aid of a grid. Each square on the page equals 1cm. Cut a piece of 1cm graph paper 51 x 35cm. Copy the pattern onto the graph paper by marking the points where the stocking pattern crosses a grid line. Draw a line joining all the points together.

FREE MACHINE EMBROIDERY

Several projects in this book require free machine embroidery and a simple guide is given here. Many books are available which will give more detailed information and guidance on the subject.

Machine embroidery is great fun to do and some beautiful effects can be achieved. Never see machine embroidery as a quick way of imitating hand stitchery. It has a character all of its own and, with experimentation and practice, you will discover that a variety of textures and patterns can be obtained with simple adjustments to tension and using different threads.

It is important that you check your machine to make sure that it can be adapted for free stitchery. Most modern machines are suitable. There are three basic adjustments to make:

1 Remove the foot.
2 Lower the dog feed, or cover with a metal plate.
3 Set the stitch length to zero.

An embroidery hoop is used for free embroidery. Bind the inner ring with tape or bias binding to ensure a good grip on the fabric that is to be worked.

Place the fabric over the outer ring. Position the inner ring on top, and press it firmly down inside the outer ring, securing the fabric between the two (Fig 1).

It is important for free machine embroidery that the fabric is very taut in the hoop. The tension screw can be tightened for extra grip.

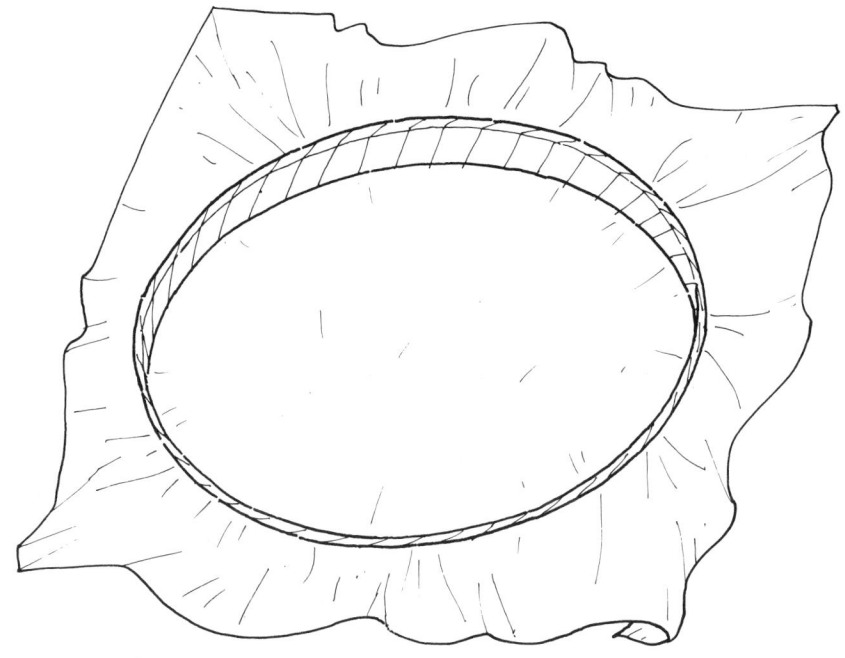

Fig 1 Showing fabric mounted in a loop ready for free machine embroidery

STARTING MACHINING

Place the hoop under the needle and lower the presser foot lever.

Try to keep your body in a relaxed posture. Place your hands lightly on either side of the hoop. Bring the bobbin thread to the surface of the fabric. Put the needle into the fabric by the bobbin thread and, holding the two threads away from you, begin stitching. Start with a few stitches on top of each other to secure the threads which can then be cut off. The length of the stitches is determined by the speed of the machine – slowly for short stitches, fast for long ones. Practice will show you what can be achieved by altering the speed and moving the hoop.

USING ZIGZAG STITCH

1   Keep the stitch length at zero.
2   Set the machine to zigzag.
3   Select a stitch width.

Interesting effects can be achieved using a zigzag stitch for free embroidery. It is particularly useful as a filling stitch when rows are worked close together (also when rows are worked over and into each other).

A row of straight stitch can be couched with a row of zigzag to give a slightly raised effect.

MACHINE CUTWORK WITH A LACE FILLING

Take a square of firmly woven fabric and draw a small circle in the centre. Place in an embroidery hoop, making sure that the tension is tight.

Set the machine for free embroidery. Work a row of straight stitching round the edge of the circle. (Fig 1).

Cut away the circle close to the stitching. Still using straight stitch, start at one side of the circle, point A anchoring the stitches firmly. Moving slowly, machine across the circle to the other side and attach at point B. Machine round the circle to point C and repeat the procedure to point D (Fig 2).

Work as many bars as required.

The bars can be made more prominent with a row of zigzag couched over the straight stitch.

An attractive filling can be achieved by machining round the central point where the bars meet (Fig 3). Having finished the spiral, bring the stitching back to the fabric to secure before cutting off the threads.

Finish off the edge of the circle with a row of zigzag.

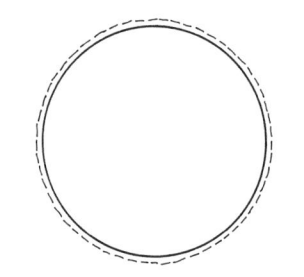

Fig 1 Showing the stitching round the circle

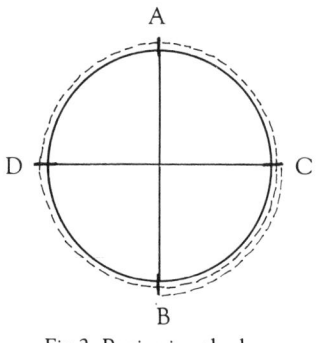

Fig 2 Beginning the bars

Fig 3 Showing the finished filling

STITCHES

Back stitch

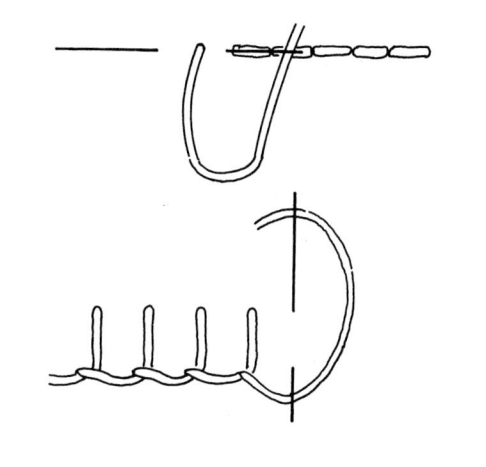

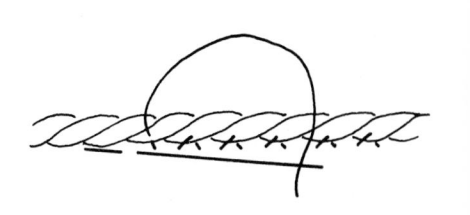

Slip stitching a cord. Make short stitches into both sides of the cord so that they are hidden in the twists of the cord

Blanket stitch

Cross stitch

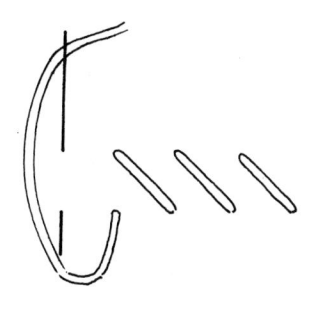

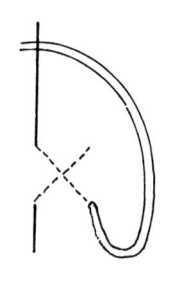

Featherstitch

Couching a cord. Couching is a method of tying down one or several threads with another. Threads to be couched are laid on the surface of the material and held in place while the couching stitches are worked at regular intervals along the laid threads

Thorn stitch

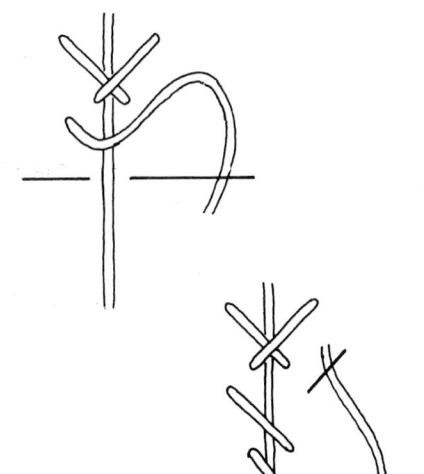

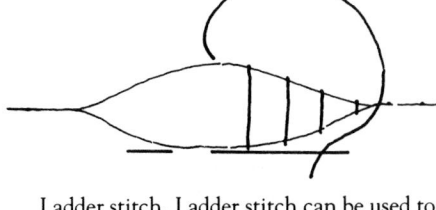

Ladder stitch. Ladder stitch can be used to invisibly bring the two sides of an opening together

TASSEL

Cut a piece of card the required depth of the tassel. Wind threads round the card as many times as is necessary to make the thickness needed for the finished tassel.

Take a needle and thread under the top of the wound threads and tie securely (Fig 1).

Cut the lower threads to release from the card (Fig 2).

With both ends of the tying thread in the needle, take the needle down through the tassel threads and out at about 12mm (½in).

Bind several times round the neck, then take the thread back through the binding and up to the top where the thread can be used to sew onto the article (Fig 3).

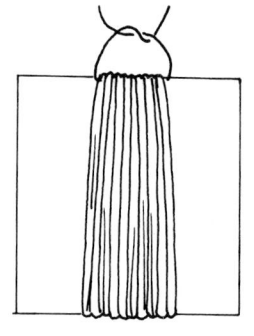

Fig 1 Threads wound round the card

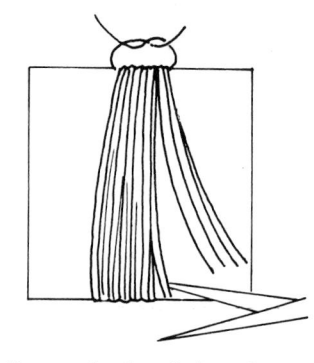

Fig 2 Cutting the threads from the card

Fig 3 Finished tassel

TEMPLATES

It is important to make accurate templates. Trace the pattern off the page using greaseproof or tracing paper or photocopy the patterns. Include any 'leave open' marks etc on the tracing.

Transfer the patterns to thin card by one of the following methods:

1   Stick the tracing to the card – spray adhesive is very good for this.
2   Use a soft pencil to draw over all the lines on the back of the tracing. Place right side up on the card and draw along the lines again with a sharp pencil.
3   Use dressmaker's carbon paper. Place the paper between the card and the tracing and draw over the lines with a sharp pencil.

Cut out the templates carefully. Curved scissors are helpful when cutting difficult inward curves.

TWISTED CORD

The illustrations show the making of a cord, with one person, using a hook.

Measure a length of thread three times the required length of the finished cord. If a heavier cord is required, add more threads.

Tie the ends of the threads together and loop over a hook. Insert a pencil through the loop at the opposite end (Fig 1).

Hold the threads firmly round the pencil and begin twisting it away from you, keeping the line under tension all the time (this is very important).

You will see the twist increasing along the line. Continue until a kink appears when the tension is released a fraction. The twist will then be sufficient (Fig 2).

Keeping the tension taut all the time, take hold of the centre of the line and double back, bringing the pencil to the hook (Fig 3). If it is a very long cord, someone else must help to hold the centre.

Now slide your hand down the cord and gradually release the tension at short intervals and the threads will twist together evenly (Fig 4).

Tie both ends together and the cord is complete.

The twisting process is quicker if one person stands at each end of the tied threads. They must face each other and twist the pencil in a clockwise direction.

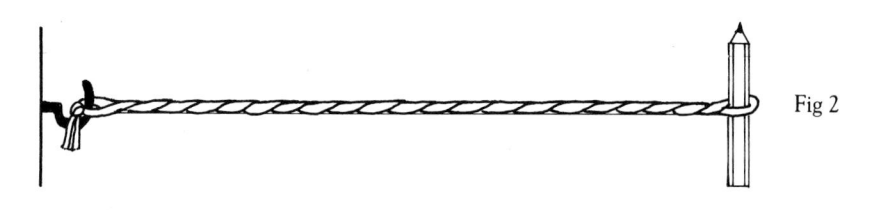

Fig 1

Fig 2

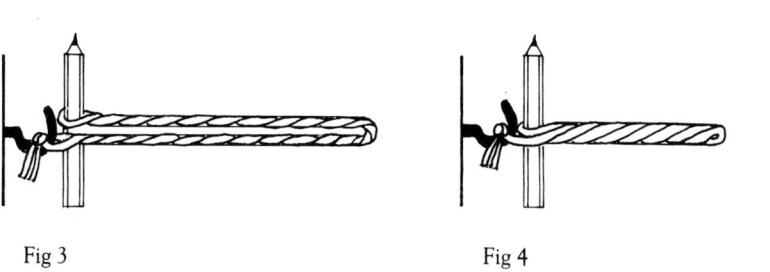

Fig 3   Fig 4

INDEX

☆

David Gentleman's illustration of Boxkite on military manoeuvres from *Bristol Fashion*, published to mark BAC's 50th anniversary in 1960 (reproduced by permission of the artist).

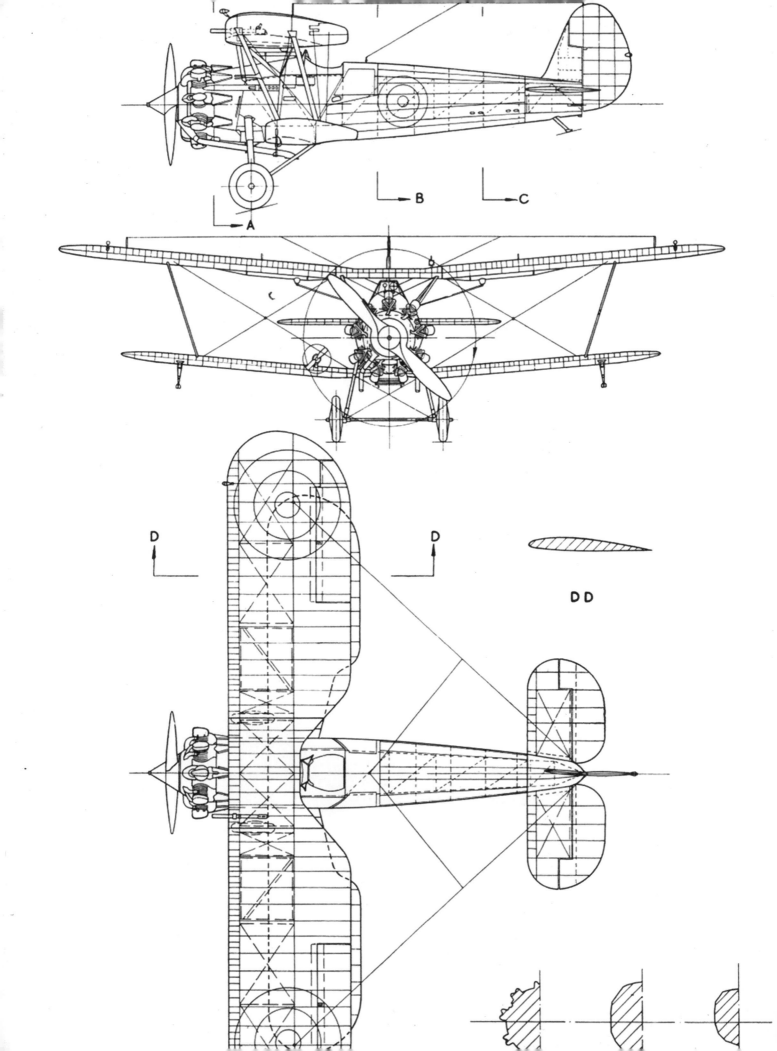